# Acclaim for *REPAIR Your Life*

"When we found the model for our woman's support group, *The Lamplighters*, and the program *REPAIR*, we were thrilled. It is exactly what was desperately needed in International Falls and Koochiching County. We have now expanded our support group to include women of Fort Frances and the surrounding area in Ontario, Canada. After finding Marjorie McKinnon and the support she offered, we are now into our program. Our first meeting was a huge success. Thank you Marjorie and God bless you for adapting this program for our survivors to follow. You have given survivors hope to continue on their healing journey."

—Donna Gustafson, Executive Director,
*Sunrise Center Against Sexual Abuse*

"I just feel very touched this morning because I am reading your *REPAIR* book for adults. It is wonderful and is helping me in my work with DV survivors. I just want to tell you that you are an amazing woman and I want to thank you for sharing your story, life and truth in this book. I feel honored to know you, and like you, am dedicated to helping other women have and find their voice."

—Monteze Deputy, Victim Advocate

"...a magnificent book, written with such understanding of the pain a child goes through and the gates that are needed to get through and enter in order to heal. Such love and thought goes into this book of healing. I highly recommend it to anyone who has ever experienced this kind of abuse."

—Cheryl Newton-Boyer, Lamplighter Facilitator

"As a practicing Marriage Family Therapist for almost twenty years in California, and as a recovering woman from the effects of childhood sexual abuse, I am delighted to write this letter of recommendation. Marjorie McKinnon's book, *REPAIR Your Life*, is logically constructed and sensitively presented. The author employs didactic and experiential learning in a clear manner which invites the reader to risk dealing with the scars of childhood sexual abuse and incest.

REPAIR, when used as an adjunct to therapy and/or support groups, offers 'hands-on' exercises which will facilitate and hasten the process of healing. I have personal experience with many of the tools the author presents and can attest to their usefulness. Anyone wanting to recover from the life-long trauma of childhood sexual abuse will benefit from this book. *REPAIR Your Life* will become the reader's wise and trusted companion along the road to wellness."

—Marcelle B. Taylor, MFT

"As a counseling psychologist who often works with people who had suffered sexual abuse as children, I find every recommendation in this book to be valid. This program just has to work, because, whether intuitively or through research, Marjorie McKinnon has assembled a highly effective program of recovery. Editing this book has been an honor. I hope it is read by all those many people who desperately need it."

—Robert Rich, PhD, www.BobsWriting.com

# REPAIR
## YOUR LIFE

A Program for Recovery from
Incest & Childhood Sexual Abuse

Marjorie McKinnon

REPAIR Your Life: A Program for Recovery from Incest &
Childhood Sexual Abuse
Copyright © 2008 Marjorie McKinnon. All Rights Reserved

First Edition: June 2008

Library of Congress Cataloging-in-Publication Data

McKinnon, Marjorie, 1942-
  Repair your life : a program of recovery from incest & childhood
sexual abuse / Margie McKinnon. -- 1st ed.
     p. cm. -- (New horizons in therapy series)
  Includes bibliographical references and index.
  ISBN-13: 978-1-932690-52-1 (trade paper : alk. paper)
  ISBN-10: 1-932690-52-2 (trade paper : alk. paper)
  1. Adult child sexual abuse victims--Rehabilitation. 2. Incest vic-
tims--Rehabilitation. I. Title.
  RC569.5.A28M394 2008
  616.85'83690651--dc22
                                        2008009239

Published by:
Loving Healing Press
5145 Pontiac Trail
Ann Arbor, MI 48105
USA

http://www.LovingHealing.com or
info@LovingHealing.com
Fax +1 734 663 6861

LovingHealingPress

# Table of Contents

Table of Figures ......................................................... iv

Introduction ............................................................. vii

Chapter 1 – Marjorie's Story................................. 1

  A Program called R.E.P.A.I.R............................ 13

Chapter 2 – Overview.................................... 15

  The Rewards for Completing REPAIR .................... 22

Chapter 3 – Recognition ............................... 31

Chapter 4 – Entry ....................................... 53

Chapter 5 – Process ..................................... 69

  Tips To Help You In The Midst Of Your Journey .... 94

Chapter 6 – Awareness ............................... 103

Chapter 7 – Insight .................................... 119

Chapter 8 – Rhythm................................... 135

Chapter 9 – Post-Recovery ......................... 149

Appendix – Resources ............................... 161

  The Desiderata by Max Ehrmann...................... 161

  The Twelve Steps ...................................... 163

  The Serenity Prayer ................................... 164

  The Optimist's Creed ................................. 165

  Support Groups........................................ 167

Bibliography ............................................ 171

About the Author...................................... 175

Index .................................................... 177

# Table of Figures

A Program called R.E.P.A.I.R. ................................... 13

Fig. 2-1: The Wounded Child ............................... 18

Fig. 2-2: A Hole in the Soul ................................ 20

Fig. 2-3: The Bridge of Recovery ....................... 21

Fig. 2-4: A Woman in Prison ............................... 22

Fig. 4-1: The Twelve Steps ................................. 58

Fig. 4-2: Rules for Good Sleep ........................... 66

Fig. 5-1: The Magic Mirror ................................ 73

Fig. 5-2: The Family Tree .................................. 90

Fig. 5-3: Tips to help you in the midst of your journey
........................................................................ 94

Fig. 5-4: Boundary Setting ................................. 97

Fig. 6-1: Properties of Awareness ...................... 103

Fig. 6-2: Family System Checklist ...................... 107

Fig. 6-3: Co-dependency Symptoms Checklist ........ 110

Fig. 7-1: Throwing Baggage Away ...................... 128

Fig. 8-1: Mountains turning into rocks, rocks into
pebbles .......................................................... 142

Fig. 9-1: Post-Recovery Worksheet ..................... 155

To my children,
Catherine, Tammie,
Michael & Teri

The greatest joy I've ever known

If you are happy
and your life is working well,
you don't need this book.

If the partner you are with
treats you with care and respect,
and your world is peopled with those
who make healthy choices,
you don't need this book.

If you have no
dark and painful shadows
from your childhood
lurking in the corners of your mind,
you don't need this book.

# Introduction

I am a non-professional whose only credentials are my personal journey through incest recovery. Several years ago, I realized that someone who had walked the same road could prove to be a sensitive and pragmatic resource for those who are trying to heal. I know so well what goes on inside the heart, the mind and the soul of one who has been sexually abused as a child.

My program, REPAIR, is the result of several years of note-taking, journalizing, meditation, and piecing together parts of my own life, as well as conversations with other incest survivors across the country. As I worked my way through recovery, I kept notes in anticipation that someday what I was learning might help others. When I began this book, I re-read my own first-person account, *Let Me Hurt You and Don't Cry Out,* to re-walk the path I had taken. I never realized at the time how blessed I was, for that path, although rugged, was straight, and in retrospect provided me with invaluable help to create this program.

I have met many incest survivors during my years of recovery, both locally and in traveling to other states. Everywhere I've been, I talked about what I was going through. It proved to be a catharsis. Initially, people were shocked that I spoke of what had happened so openly, and as if it were not my fault. My comment, "It wasn't," at first proved startling. Little by little, I noticed that others came forward with their stories. Sometimes they spoke in hushed whispers, giving furtive looks as if they might be punished. Other times, they spoke boldly, trying to escape from a prison. When I asked questions and responded with sympathy, they became more daring:

now giving details, talking of feelings, often sharing about others they knew who had also survived. I tracked coincidences, made notes on their needs and their pain, and asked questions about resources available in their areas and what it might take to make them whole again.

When I began the outline for the program, I knew that it cried out for a title that aptly described what needed to be done. *Repair* was the first word that came to my mind. It literally means to restore by replacing a part or putting together what is torn or broken; to restore to a sound or healthy state. What better word describes our goal in the case of childhood sexual abuse? In particular, I knew that it wasn't enough to rid ourselves of the pain; we needed to fill the void with something good. I also knew that the ultimate reward was making healthy choices and living a life free from the despair that kept us bound by dark shadows, doomed to live in a three-sided prison.

After spending a year with my initial therapist, I was on my own. Although I eventually found another, most of my success in recovery was due to following my own instincts and wading through the trial and error of many different groups, seminars, books, and CDs. The techniques that I devised, some of which I had no idea at the time would contribute monumentally to getting healthy, were fine-tuned. Developing the stages came naturally as I thought back on what had happened during the five years that I was in both recovery and post recovery.

*** 

Most of us have learned ways over the years to cope with depression, emotional pain and shadowy memories that bring anxiety. Some of you are saying, *I'm still angry, but my life is OK.* But is it? In this program you're going to ask yourself some hard questions. Hopefully, by the end of it you'll see things more clearly.

If you don't need this program or one like it, I'm happy for you. I wish no one did. Few people who were sexually violated at a young age are able to go through life without getting help and still be happy. My goal is to help you heal, help you move away from the past, and give you tools to make adjustments so that your life can be everything you want it to be. I've been where you were and my life changed forever because of it. Now, I'd like you to be who I am today, the happiest person I know.

# 1 Marjorie's Story

I'm going to begin this book with a story. Mine. Hopefully, everyone reading will identify with parts of it and realize they're in the right place. We all have stories that are different. We all have stories that are the same. Repercussions in the life of an incest victim ripple like waves in a body of water, ones that eventually turn into riptides, undercurrents and sometimes tidal waves.

My story is a classic example.

In July of 1988, I walked into the office of therapist Marci Taylor, a specialist in the field of childhood sexual abuse. The damage done by my incest had accelerated to the point of despair. It was six months before my third marriage and I had a long history of relationships with alcoholics and abusers, two of them former husbands. Suicidal since my early teens, I had been hospitalized for two nervous breakdowns in my twenties, one the result of a failed suicide attempt. I had hidden my pain behind too much alcohol, promiscuity, compulsive behavior, obsessive relationships and extremes of emotional highs and lows. Only medication, intermittently taken, had kept me functioning for almost twenty-five years.

Two years earlier, I had been engaged to my daughter's father-in-law. Chuck was the first healthy male in my life, a man whose primary aim was making me happy. He became convinced that something traumatizing had happened in my childhood that I didn't remember. His comment, "How could someone as wonderful as you wind up with so many abusive men," not only went right over my head, but irritated me as he be-

gan a personal crusade to find out what had happened. I
retaliated with anger, tried to end the engagement, and
when he refused, began an affair outside the relationship. His response was, "I'll never leave you except
through death." Within months, he was diagnosed with
lung cancer. Filled with shame and fear for Chuck, I
ended the affair and took care of him while he was ill.
Even then, a few days before he died, still unable to control my own sexual addiction, I slept not only with
another man, but a married one. After Chuck's death my
guilt and shame at what I had done caused despair so
great I wished only that I had never failed in my many
suicide attempts.

Within a few weeks, I was living with the man who
would ultimately set off a trail of such severe abuse that
I had to choose between death and entering recovery. I
had hit bottom. Having read my private journals without
permission, he used my descriptions of previous lovers
and infidelities as a whip to taunt me, especially the
night I had spent in bed with a married man while
Chuck lay dying. Like Pavlov's dog, every time he rang
the bell by shaming me about my past, I obeyed whatever his current demand was, for I learned quickly that
giving in caused the torment to cease. Subject to his
whims, I lived like a prisoner, crippled by his several-
times-a-day sexual addiction—which quickly turned into
brutal rapes—his need to control what I wore, who I
spoke with, what I said, and even whether I laughed or
not.

Within months, my beautiful home looked like a bat-
tleground, with bathroom doors he had split in half
when I cowered behind them hiding from his rages and
sexual obsessions, broken furniture and holes in walls,

all evidence of my out-of-control emotions from the terror of his rapes. Once he forced me into making sex video-tapes by taunting me about previous infidelities. In the process, I lost my mind as I lay in a fetal position on the floor calling for my mother. Before we'd been together a year, his need for frequent middle-of-the-night sex was causing painful and confusing flashbacks.

One time, years earlier, in the office of a therapist, I had spied a cartoon. It was of a woman standing in a cage with her hands clenched on the bars, looking out-ward with terror. The cage had only three sides. That cartoon was so painful that I averted my eyes every time I saw it. It haunted me for years, and became one of the spurs to my entering recovery, for now I could see that I was that woman.

My self-image was so poor that once, in a department store, I saw a woman on the other side of the room and thought desperately, *I would give anything if only I looked like her.* As I walked closer, I realized that her body movements matched mine. I'd been staring in a mirror! Even then, I waved my arms and made faces, then finally touched the glass before I became convinced it was me. You'd think it would have caused me to look at myself in a different light. It didn't. I wasn't ready to believe that there was anything beautiful about me. Even my frequent quip over the years, "If you took sex out of my life, I'd be a near-perfect person," did not encourage me to see that although I had a dark side, there were many gems beneath my surface.

Despite the use of various therapists over the years who had probed my life, none had ever identified incest as the culprit. In my early thirties, my father had admit-ted to his wrongdoing, making the comment, "It really wasn't so bad, kiddo, they do it in the Appalachian district all the time." Shortly before he died, he again brought it up, then abruptly dropped it. Both times I buried the reality, the pain too monumental to consider. I was not even sure what the word "incest" meant and other than a nightmare I'd had when I was younger, one where a steamroller was suffocating me as I lay in my bottom bunk, I had no memory of such things happening. I had relived the "nightmare" hundreds of times throughout my life, on each occasion waking up screaming as I felt the paralyzing terror of being overpowered by an unknown force. The nightmares didn't cease until after my father's death in 1985.

Now, shaking with continuous tremors, I turned once more to therapy. This time it was at the insistence of my family doctor, who had been convinced for many years that incest was the source of my problems.

Marci began my treatment with several sessions of discussions concerning my childhood. I gave her the same story I had given the others. I was the oldest daughter in a Midwestern Catholic family. My father had delivered me in the middle of a blizzard in northern Minnesota. As the years went by, his interest in me became obsessive. My mother, worn down from having four children in as many years, turned her fifth child, a daughter, over to me to raise. At the age of eight, I had become the family housekeeper and at the age of nine, a mother. When I was thirteen I had the "nightmare" that was to haunt me for so many years.

For reasons I didn't understand at the time, during this period our family life changed dramatically. Mom and Dad discarded any semblance of love and togetherness. My siblings and I became like mutilated soldiers in the midst of a war, as we wandered through our days in a continual state of anxiety and terror of Dad. He began a crusade to prove me no good, referring to me as "unclean." Most of the time Mom lay in bed sobbing or in an alcoholic-like stupor where she had me shave her legs, bathe her, and care for her as if she were in the midst of a debilitating illness. I spiraled into despair, becoming not only manic depressive, but suicidal.

I had come from a long line of patriarchal families with fathers who had a strong sense of their own importance and mothers who subjugated their needs to those of the head of the family. We walked on eggs if Dad was in the house, lest we offend in some way. His word was not only law, but any opinions contrary to his were punishable. This way of life duplicated my father's growing-up years as well as my mother's. It felt normal to me. My mother's motto was: *Even when your father is wrong, he's right.* A few years later she developed breast cancer, and Dad convinced her that all doctors were quacks, depriving her of the medical care that might have saved her life. She died angry, resentful, and confused about her own value system.

At the age of 18, after a beating from my father that almost killed me, I stuffed a few belongings into a pillowcase and ran. Once on my own, I entered what was to become more than thirty years of unhealthy choices and abusive relationships.

After hearing the story of my life and descriptions of my current victimization, Marci gave me an assignment. I was to draw pictures at various intervals of my life with my left hand, depicting emotions in different colors. I found the exercise rather silly until I sat at the kitchen table and began drawing. There, memories I had forgot-

ten surfaced. When I got to the age of 13, I drew a picture of a young girl lying on a bottom bunk bed. A gray
haired man stood in the doorway. I grabbed a red crayon
and wrote: *Help me! Help me!* across the face of it, before
bursting into tears.

Within days, I entered a twelve-step program, and
through hypnosis and more therapy sessions with Marci,
began to see the truth, not only of what had happened to
me, but the impact it had on my life and the kind of decisions I had made. At the age of thirteen, I had become
my father's unwilling mistress. Eventually, my mother
discovered Dad's middle-of-the-night rapes while I slept
with a rosary clutched in my hand. Unable to deal with
the thought that her husband was the perpetrator of
such a crime, she made me the scapegoat, frequently
taunting my father into beating me with a belt. Even
those memories were never defined in my head as child
abuse, only as strict parenting.

Recovery, prolonged by my decision to stay with my
abuser, lasted for almost five years. It was like trying to
swim upstream with heavy chains hanging around my
neck. I worked a rigorous and honest twelve-step program, attended seminars on child abuse and self-esteem,
read recovery books, listened to recovery CDs, chronicled
my life story, journalized on a regular basis, constructed
a "Magic Mirror" (you will find out more about this later),
and traveled out of state to meet my father's relatives,
then pieced together the family history that had set me
up for self-destruction. In short, I did all the things that I
later utilized in developing REPAIR.

As I traveled across what I had begun calling the
Bridge of Recovery, tools were periodically placed in my
path, to not only see the truth, but to empower me. Later

on in the program, I will more fully describe this bridge. I recall the day my daughter gave me a workbook entitled *I Never Knew I had a Choice.* The title alone set off gratifying leaps in behavior changes. Another time, while shopping at a swap meet, I found a sweatshirt that proclaimed "What part of NO don't you understand?" Whenever I wore it, I felt stronger. A brochure in a pharmacist's office stated, "Losing your freedom of choice is a bitter pill to swallow." It caused me to sob for days until I finally tapped into a new truth. It was all the start, at first in baby steps, to not only saying no when an unhealthy choice was offered, but realizing that I could make my own healthy choices.

In the middle of my recovery, my youngest daughter inadvertently commented on what had happened sexually to her sisters when they were little. I froze with terror and within minutes, after calling my two older daughters, discovered that they too had been "incested" by my second husband while we were married. Grief strangled me as my need to become totally healthy accelerated in the hope that it would change the lives of my children. As I thought of my grandchildren and their children, a sense of urgency overwhelmed me. It was only later that I found out that children of an untreated incest victim stand a five times greater chance of being incested themselves, because incest is a multi-generational illness. This knowledge compounded my guilt.

My eldest daughter, alcoholic and bulimic, had already duplicated my penchant for going from man to man. One of her sisters had spent ten years in a nightmare marriage to a violent and unstable man. To add to the burden was my despair that I may have contributed in some way to my youngest daughter, at seventeen, being raped at gunpoint by a masked bandit. She too, was currently married to a man who was so abusive that one time he pointed a gun to her head and forced her to relive her rape.

I staggered at the realization that four out of five of my family members were victims of sexual abuse. To make the statistics more ironic, my son was an officer on the Los Angeles Police Department (LAPD). He had never been sexually abused and was happily married, stable, and disciplined. He not only made healthy choices on a regular basis, it was difficult for him to understand why others didn't. On the day he graduated from the LAPD, he had hugged me and said, "I think I can make a difference, Mom." His words placed a balance in the midst of my torment. I could only hope that his career choice would one day save others from perpetrators.

In October of 1992, I journeyed back to the small town where I had been molested and raped by my father. There, armed with the courage of four and a half years of recovery, I confronted the ghosts from my past by going into my former bedroom. Although it was the hardest thing I have ever done, it empowered me. I came home, forced my abuser out of the house, got a restraining order against him, filed for a divorce, and spent the next six months doing post-recovery work.

Today, I can hardly remember what it feels like to be suicidal. Periodically, and with a certain wry humor, I ask my Higher Power to "please disregard previous instructions." Today I make healthy choices and am filled with a sense of wonder and enchantment. I am strong, centered, stable, joyful, disciplined, and self-sufficient. My shame is a thing of the past, and despair and hopelessness are no longer a part of my life. I still experience sad times and stress, but now I have the right tools to handle any problems that arise. Today the motto above my desk reads: *If I had known life was going to turn out this good, I would have started it earlier.*

No matter how painful your past, how filled with shame your life has been, it is never too late to change. Fifty years ago, "incest" was a word few people knew. Those who did thought it was biblical in origin and certainly had nothing to do with what Dad or grandpa or Uncle Willy was doing to us in the middle of the night. Today, so much help is available that no one needs to suffer. All it takes is the right program and the commitment to follow it. It won't be easy. Most things of value have a price. But the price is small compared to the waiting reward. The journey itself, arduous though it may be, will awaken your frightened inner child. It will teach her (or him) emotionally healthy behavior and validate lost treasures, those parts to ourselves we've been unable to see.

When I was in recovery, I heard a lot about the "inner child." It was not an unknown expression. In 1963, Dr. W. Hugh Missildine had written a best seller entitled *Your Inner Child of the Past.* I had read it in the '70s but, of course, it had nothing to do with me. Even then, the inner child concept was not as deeply explored as it became later, primarily by John Bradshaw.

As I progressed across my Bridge of Recovery, I thought more and more about my inner child. Was there actually such a creature? Since my early teens, I had heard a screaming voice within. I assumed that everyone had this screaming voice. Now I wondered. Could that be my inner child? About two years before I entered recovery, I purchased a doll with no face. I had no way of knowing that my desire to have one without a face was because I couldn't see the real me. Halfway through recovery, as the light at the end of that bridge became visible, I searched for a doll with a face. I found her at an arts and crafts festival. Not only did she have a face, it was a happy one. When I turned her over and wound the key on her back, she played, "We've only just begun." I'd found the symbol I needed to begin exploring my inner self for that child.

One day as I sat on a swing in a nearby park, I spoke out loud to my imaginary child. I wasn't sure I believed in her but the doll on my bed haunted me. What if there was a child? What if she was waiting for me to reach out and comfort her? Hesitantly, I continued speaking. I told her I was sorry I had put her through so much. I apologized for not listening to the screaming voice. I said, in almost a whisper, that I was working on getting well and I promised that one day she would no longer scream, she would no longer cry, she would be the happy face. All of a sudden, I felt as if a little girl had stepped out of the shadows, her tearstained face staring up at me. I began sobbing and literally reached down and wrapped my arms around her as we both wept.

During the next few months, I spent many mornings at that park while we swung together. She told me about the time the bullies in the school yard had thrown rocks at her for what she was wearing. I consoled her about the loss of her first love in the fifth grade, a boy named Jerry Bennett. From there we grieved over the loss of her mother, the loneliness and despair of her teen years, the scars of her siblings and the early and tragic death of her baby sister. Together we explored all the moments, and as the months continued to pass, she stopped crying, stopped wearing a mournful look, and after my recovery ended, laughed and played. Today, my inner child and I connect immediately whenever I am involved in activities she likes best—swinging on swings, sliding down slides, climbing trees and hiking in the woods, all activities that, despite being the grandmother of fourteen and the great-grandmother of two, I do with relish.

As you move through recovery you will find your inner child growing emotionally as a new-found maturity develops in both of you. The frightened child you once were becomes an adult who is capable of being child-like, but not childish. This change brings great inner strength.

The concept of this inner child may seem silly to you as it once did to me. But she is very real in each one of you. She is that innocent child before the time of trauma. She is waiting for you to begin recovery, to rescue her from that dark place where she has lived for so many years. Don't turn your back on her. I promise that once you reach the other side of the bridge, your joy in life will be overwhelming.

To enhance the happy ending to my story, in 1995 my oldest daughter, Cathy, committed herself to an addictive disorder center for 30 days for alcoholism. A year later Cathy and her husband had Emily Rose, the first child in my family to be born to a treated victim of childhood sexual abuse. In October of 2005, Cathy celebrated ten years of sobriety.

As time passed and I made wiser choices, I also saw a pronounced difference in the choices my other daughters made. Although they are not yet in recovery, both have rid themselves of their abusers. As you can see, a treated incest victim can influence the lives of her children a great deal. Today, I see them making positive changes and mature decisions, and for the first time since they became adults, my daughters are leading happier lives.

As for me, my days are rich and filled with joy. In May of 2000, I married another McKinnon, a mountain man named Tom from the Colorado Rockies whom I met through the Internet during a genealogy search. We were married at Melrose Abbey in Melrose, Scotland with bagpipers playing at a reception that included a number of friends we've made from the United Kingdom. Tom is gentle, kind, full of personal integrity and cherishes me as I deserve. Today we live near Sedona, Arizona, a dream I'd had for many years.

Chuck, the man who died of cancer, and I have three grandchildren together, two of them born after his death. I had promised him before he died that I would tell his grandchildren about him so they would know him as I did. Until I moved to Colorado, every year on the anniversary of his birthday, Michael, Hunter, and Katie Montana wrote letters to the grandfather they never knew. Together we visited his grave, where they put flowers on his headstone and read to him the letters they'd written. Wherever Chuck is, I feel he has forgiven me as I have forgiven myself.

# A Program called R.E.P.A.I.R.

While the Bridge of Recovery is a visual tool,
the Program is a map to take you across that bridge.

## The Stages

| | |
|---|---|
| **Recognition** | Recognizing and accepting that your adult problems stem from childhood sexual abuse. |
| **Entry** | Entering a program of commitment to change your life for the better. |
| **Process** | Learning tools and techniques that will enable you to become healthy. |
| **Awareness** | The coming together of reality as you gather the pieces of the broken puzzle your life became, and begin assembling them to see the complete picture. Here you discover the properties of awareness that were God-given promises at birth, lost at the moment of sexual abuse. |
| **Insight** | Seeing the complete picture and beginning to return to what you were prior to being sexually violated. |
| **Rhythm** | Developing the natural rhythm you had before the incest happened, the blueprint that is the essence of your true nature, becoming who you really are. |

| **2** | **Overview** |  |

We are born and we die.
Somewhere between those two major events
Lie opportunities to be and do all that we want.
It's not a difficult goal...

*Unless you were sexually molested as a child.*

Webster defines incest as "sexual intercourse between persons too closely related to marry legally." It is a simple, almost clinical description that does not in any way imply trauma or abuse. The all-encompassing and often unspoken reality is much broader. Anyone in a position of power who coerces a person of lesser power into any sort of boundary violation dealing with their sexuality, either emotionally, mentally, or physically, is a sexual abuse perpetrator. This includes a grandfather who pins his granddaughter down while he fondles her breasts; a father who insists on watching his daughter, against her wishes, while she bathes; an older brother who forces his sister to do oral sex; and any other such boundary violations from the most minor to actual forcible entry and rape. It does not have to be a family member to have the same resultant despair. That despair, whether by a family member or an outsider, can be a life sentence of pain.

No one would willingly choose a painful life. But sometimes early victimization leads us down a path where all we experience is the dark side. Negativity, which has an actual energy field, contains great power and once it grabs hold, is not easily removed. Neither are the wounds that incest causes.

Wounded to her very soul, if not treated, an incest victim either stumbles through a life of despair or dies from it. The tragedy of incest is that, unlike a physical wound, the aftermath can spread to the children, who in turn are either sexually abused or begin a lifetime of un-healthy choices, the direct result of a poor self-image created from shame.

Guilt is the driving force that causes this shame and erodes our self-esteem. A child is egocentric, and there-fore perceives all that happens to him as an event he has created and is therefore responsible for. A sexually abused child experiences the humiliation and degrada-tion of shame in a monumental way. He senses the need to keep it secret, thereby creating more shame. If one could but talk about the pain, incest could be brought into the open and exposed as the real enemy, but hu-miliation keeps him from speaking the truth. Perpetrators know this, and use that secrecy as a way to protect themselves, and diminish their wrongdoing. They look for the following qualities in their victims: obedi-ence, weak boundaries, innocence and naiveté, as well as someone smaller and easy to manipulate.

Childhood sexual abuse has nothing to do with sex. It is an act of violence with its origins in the need for power and control. In many cases the perpetrator was abused himself as a child and is acting out what was perpetrated on him. As an adult, he may become the abusive partner in domestic violence and his mate someone who has made victimization a way of life.

As for the sexually abused person often trapped in this cycle, what began as a joyful child becomes a hu-man being who must hide her real self; hence alcohol, drugs, promiscuity, overeating and compulsive behavior develop, all designed to create self-loathing. As the years pass, the victim piles shame upon shame with unhealthy choices; his or her self-image spirals into an all time low. But we are not the sum total of what we have done. It is necessary during recovery to separate what we have done from who we are, to see that we are not a body with a soul, we are a soul with a body. No matter what has been done to our body, no one can ever touch the soul. It remains pure and innocent. Once we arrive at that realization, we begin to let go of the shame.

Since, after being sexually abused, our self-worth plunges, it is almost impossible to pull out of the negative energy field that has been established and enter one of positive energy. If you add a non-supportive, co-dependent parent, a society that doesn't want to hear about sexual abuse, and an environment that encourages a lack of boundary setting, the continuing of a life of negativity is almost guaranteed.

We all know what it feels like to get out of bed on the wrong side and how it colors our entire day. Incest victims get out of bed on the wrong side every day. They may learn how to hide and deny it, but it's always with them, lurking somewhere in the shadows. "I've learned how to live with it," is a comment I've frequently heard. Why should anyone learn how to live with something as if it were a disease that they could do nothing about, especially when there is an option to heal? Most of the time, child sexual abuse victims are unaware that they have the power to change their own life. Unable to see the light, they become comfortable with the pain.

People with low self-esteem feel they don't deserve the wonderful opportunities available in life. When one presents itself, it is almost as if a master puppeteer pulls our strings and causes us to veer off the path that could have proven a way out of our torment. Most sexual abuse victims move through their days as if that puppeteer were an inescapable part of their lives.

If you can take this negative energy field and, through the use of REPAIR, turn it into a positive one, it will impact the lives around you. This includes your children, and also every other human you touch. Like the reverse of an epidemic—and incest is at epidemic proportions—the light of REPAIR has the potential to change the direction of mankind. Positive (or healthy) energy repairs and negative (or unhealthy) energy destroys. The negative energy of one person can impact an entire room and what's worse, an entire day.

wounded child

A wounded child attracts negative people. Somehow, adults who were sexually abused as children find perpetrators as mates, codependents pair off with alcoholics, bullies find waiting victims, and obedient people wind up with controlling partners. The good news is that once you complete REPAIR, you'll be healthy and your ability to pull in one of a similar nature increases a thousand-fold. Doing your small part in a world that doesn't yet see the devastation of childhood sexual abuse has overwhelming rewards.

Despite being a society that is drawn to horror, intrigued with sex scandals, and compelled to watch tragedies on television, we continue to show aversion at the mention of sexual abuse. Like an ostrich burying his head in the sand, we don't want to know about such things. If truth of the sheer number of victims in our society and the far-reaching impact of their trauma was brought to bear on the majority of the population, feelings about a need to take action would change dramatically. Since sexual abuse is so prevalent, we are literally breeding a nation of children with a hole in their soul.

Recovery, in part, is about overcoming that aversion to discussing it. If we can talk openly about the troubles of alcoholism (and today we do), we can talk about incest. Not talking about it is the main reason why incest is an epidemic. When wrongdoing is not addressed, it is not dealt with, and when not dealt with, it multiplies. Silence means implied approval and creates a deadly secret, for it builds more shame into victims already overwhelmed by it.

Hole in the Soul

**Fig. 2-3: The Bridge of Recovery**

Recovery is a like a bridge you need to cross to change your life. In REPAIR, the bridge is used as a visualization tool. On one side are those things destroying you. If you turn back, depression, loneliness, despair, suicidal tendencies, addictions, shame-based low self-esteem, and fear of abandonment await you. The list is endless.

On the other side is all the good stuff. There you will find peace, healthy choices, strong self-esteem, a feeling of being centered and capable. There you will find joy. Imagine a life free from pain and emotional instability; a life where waking each morning brings happy anticipation rather than dread; a life where you can stop waiting for someone to rescue you and begin to rescue yourself. All you have to do is to keep moving across that bridge. At some point in your recovery you will learn that, like a carrot on a stick, the other side of the bridge beckons and you will no longer be tempted to turn back.

## The Rewards for Completing REPAIR

### Learning New Truths and New Behaviors

As you move through the program, it is necessary to rid yourself of the lies that kept you violated, and also to learn new truths and new behaviors. As childhood sexual abuse victims, we live in a cage of our own construction. But that cage has only three sides—one is missing but we don't know it. The thought of breaking free is not usually a luxury we allow ourselves. Freedom has a cloudy picture. It could be scary, it could be devastating. We might have to be responsible for our own actions. We might not be able to blame our sexual abuse anymore when our lives don't go in the direction we wish.

But think about the cage. Is life happy in that cage? Are we experiencing fulfillment? Why are we clutching the bars with a look of terror on our faces and our backs to the open side?

Woman in prison

## Setting Healthy Boundaries

In REPAIR, you will learn to tear down the behavior that kept you from achieving happiness, and to set healthy boundaries in areas where they are needed. While uncomfortable for a person who was sexually abused, boundaries are required for living a healthy life. Once developed and then put into practice, they will not only alleviate great stress but bring enormous personal power. Personal power is the one thing a sexually abused person never had, nor did they even realize it was one of their God-given rights. Anger used to be very dangerous. We learned that responding to upsetting events with anger brings more pain. In reality, anger its appropriate use is one of the strongest motivators to setting a boundary.

A sexual abuse victim displays the lack of personal power in various ways. One of the most prominent, knee-jerk reactions, comes from a place of fear and low self-esteem. Instead of thinking through decisions, we immediately make a choice, often not a wise one. Diametrically opposed to this is another behavior pattern of the wounded child. As we grow older, the need for self-protection causes delayed reactions to unpleasant events in our lives. Attempting to distance ourselves from the pain, we make frantic efforts to keep from feeling its full force. Learning how to set boundaries will not only empower us, it will alleviate both the knee-jerk reactions and the delayed reactions.

## Regaining Confidence

There are logical steps in the journey from shame to confidence. As we go through the program and learn that the shame is not ours, but in fact belongs to our perpetrator, we relinquish it, little by little. When this happens, we replace it with positive affirmations and other reinforcements of the truth. The various techniques taught in the Process part of REPAIR bring confidence through healthy messages and an understanding of what happened. People with confidence willingly accept responsibility for their own shortcomings and are able, when criticism comes their way, to recognize the difference between an opinion and truth. These healthy behavior patterns are nonexistent in a victim of childhood sexual abuse. We are too filled with pain to care about learning how to gain confidence.

The shame of what we have become and the behavior we use to hide it grows and is stuffed into closets in our mind. We lean our bodies against the door and turn a deaf ear to the screams that come every time we open it to hide another piece of shame. For most of us, somewhere between our late thirties and late forties, the closets in our mind fill to overflowing and we hit what Twelve Steppers call our "bottom." It is as if our life were on a course of self-destruction, one we have no ability to veer away from as we aim directly for the inevitable, unhappy endings in most areas of our lives.

## Connecting the Mind and the Heart

At birth, the heart and mind are connected, but once sexual abuse happens, they separate and the inner self splatters. Like pieces of a broken puzzle, the heart and mind fly to far corners of our inner self where they hide in fear, disconnected from each other and their ability to act as a team. Since we have not developed emotional maturity and the ability to make wise decisions, we do whatever is necessary to fumble our way through life.

During recovery, you will learn to connect the mind and heart, thereby having healthy responses. This will allow you to locate all the pieces of your unique puzzle, assemble them, and see the picture that emerges—the real you—not the one damaged by sexual abuse.

## Developing Emotional Maturity

Humans pass through stages during normal development. Each is as important as its predecessor. All stages are needed to create a healthy, responsible and vibrant human. With the loss of even one stage, we lose abilities needed to move through life in a healthy manner. A child of sexual abuse retains only the developmental stages acquired prior to the trauma. We learn to pretend we are adults. In truth, *children* raise other children, children make decisions in the workplace and, at times, children make choices that directly impact our safety and well-being.

It is an amazing experience to come to the beginning of the stage called Process and realize that you are developmentally at the same age as when you were sexually abused. It is even more amazing to feel the emotional growth begin, often in quantum leaps, as you work your way to the end of the program, through post-recovery and beyond.

## The Return of Our Original Promise of Joy

The burden lightens when we come out of the dark and begin to tell our secrets. Bits and pieces of light return, light that was taken from us at the moment of incest. As dark produces more dark, light produces more light and the joy that recovery brings multiplies, even as the despair we suffered in the beginning also multiplied.

The old saying "A sorrow shared is a sorrow halved" is true. In talking about our pain, we decrease it. On the other hand, hidden and unresolved sorrow will increase insidiously, and unless we come forward with our own truth, we will remain in a state of despair.

## Living Your Life the Way It was Intended

Einstein had an incisive definition of insanity: "Endlessly repeating the same process, hoping for a different result." The life of a victim of sexual abuse becomes insanity as we continually go down the same road, hoping for a different destination. In this program, I have used acronyms to present the stages of childhood sexual abuse recovery as a different road, one that promises only the happiest of destinations. Requiring rigorous honesty, great courage, and a sincere desire to change your life for the better, it is not for the faint-hearted.

It has been said that it takes all your life to learn how to live. This is a choice, not a mandate. Why not do it sooner? As you move toward the completion of this program, you will make tremendous progress in how to live your life the way it was meant to be.

Each of us is created in the likeness of God and are pure and innocent at birth, with a promise of fulfillment. In the case of child sexual abuse and incest, that innocence ruptures. Like a gunshot to the heart, it extracts the joy from life.

The human body has the ability to heal physically, mentally, emotionally and spiritually. The process of healing an infected wound often requires lancing. If not done immediately, the infection can spread through the body and perhaps, as in the case of gangrene, cause death. This is, figuratively speaking, what happens to a child who has been sexually molested. Once lanced, a wound will heal, eventually leaving only a faint scar. In REPAIR we are lancing the wound, but as we do so, we are applying ointment. It is not a fearful process, but it does require courage.

The purpose of this program is to send you into the world with useful tools for recovery. You will not read this book and get healed immediately. It contains exercises as well as thought provoking-questions that will plant seeds. These seeds will turn into blossoms, giving you direction and guidance in a world that at times will seem dark. Buying this book was a strong step toward simplifying the task of recovery. You must *want* to get well or you wouldn't be reading these words. And the *wanting* is the most important ingredient you will need before you start. The *wanting* will keep you balanced. It will give you purpose and strength. It will become your dearest friend during the times when you are tempted to revert to old habits, the ones that were destroying you and dragging you through a world full of darkness and quiet desperation.

***

If ever you doubt whether you are on the right path, think of your daughter or your friend's daughter or any tiny child whose eyes you have recently looked into with care and concern. Ask yourself if you can bear what happened to you happening to them. You will then come to realize that making your world safe and happy is a way of making the world safe and happy for your children and many other children. The despair that fills a sexually abused person's world touches the lives of everyone who moves within their circle.

It is vital you understand that while none of us wants to believe this could happen to our child, it often does. We are seldom aware that our children adopt behavior patterns we have, and this leads them into a trap. Qualities such as codependency, obedience, playing the victim role, and weak boundaries are only a few that we announce on an unconscious level to our children. They, in turn, believing that we are all knowing and all wise, perceive these behavior patterns as appropriate. Inadvertently they replay the role we did that attracted our original perpetrator.

We think we can protect our children by telling them to stay away from strangers. The truth is that most perpetrators are either family members or someone already known to them. We worry about extreme violence and obvious sexual assaults, when subtle kinds of force and manipulation are more likely to happen. We think that we can protect them if we ask them frequently if anyone has touched them in an inappropriate place. That won't do it. Most children will not come forward with the truth. Their shame is too overwhelming. Did you go to your non-abusive parent with the truth when it had happened to you, or did you wait for years? You can't protect your children 24 hours a day, especially as they grow older. What you can do for them is to develop new and healthy behavior learned in this program.

They will mimic you and therefore protect themselves. We've already seen what a perpetrator requires as the primary qualities in their potential victim. Being strong-minded yourself is no guarantee of protecting your child. You must teach them to be strong-minded. These truths are not meant to frighten you, but to make you aware of the need to become totally healthy as a role model for your child. Armed with this realization, isn't it time to get busy?

Life will still contain challenges after you complete REPAIR. Frogs will not automatically turn into princes, the lottery numbers won't appear on your pillow in the morning, and you will no doubt eventually have some sort of health disorder at some time in your life. However, the problems that used to be mountains will change into boulders, the boulders into rocks and the rocks into pebbles. Objectivity will set in, giving you an inner strength you never had. Instead of bonding with the pain you will detach and bond with your newly created inner strength.

You will still have good and bad days. Only, now you'll have the tools to handle the bad days. You will look ahead, *responding* to the challenges life presents instead of *reacting*.

Robert Louis Stevenson wrote in *A Child's Garden of Verse* (1889), "The world is so full of a number of things, I'm sure we should all be as happy as kings." Once you complete REPAIR, you'll look at the world through a different window. It is my hope that by then you will adopt his words as one of your mottoes.

I invite you to begin the journey that will take you across that bridge and into a whole different life, one you never thought possible. Your journey has six stages. Each one follows the other in a natural sequence as your life and the chaos it has rendered unfolds in front of you waiting to be *REPAIRED*.

| **3** | **Recognition** |  |
|:---:|:---:|:---:|

**Knowing we were sexually abused is one thing—**

*Recognizing the truth of where the blame lies,*
*and what we can do about it, is another.*

One of the things you will do in this program is gather evidence. It is necessary to see the complete picture in order to recognize the origins of your unhappy life. No one, and I repeat, *no one*, is born unhappy. It is an acquired deficiency that is a major impediment to the purpose for which you were born—a direct response to all that was done to you and your reactions to those events.

You may or may not regain any memories of being molested. To some, it is a blessing if they don't. What is important is your ability to see the truth. Only armed with the truth will you be able to move through this program and regain that state of mind into which you were born—a state of joy and high expectations of the wonderfulness that life can hand you.

The signs that indicate childhood sexual abuse as the origin of our problems are like the warning signs of cancer. They illustrate deeper problems. These problems can be mental, emotional, spiritual and physical.

We become adept at finding ways to either detach from reality (dissociation) or look the other way by creating continuous distractions. Hyper-vigilance, a condition that causes great and continuous stress, becomes a walking part of us. It interferes with our sleep, our ability to make wise decisions, and most importantly, our capacity for spontaneity and joy. It creates an environment where everyone and everything becomes suspect in the destruction of our own wellbeing. Life, instead of blossoming into the vibrant and abundant promise we expected at birth, is now a desolate affair.

The emptiness of a life filled with the baggage of untreated childhood trauma is one of the saddest things known to man. Sadder yet is the knowledge that we could have been helped. We wait with anticipation for someone to rescue us. No one had rescued us from the abuse, but somehow we think that as our lives go awry, it's only a matter of time before a knight will ride up on his steed and either protect us from life or protect us from ourselves. In our naiveté, unable to regain our own power, we fall easy prey to the abusers of the world, thereby prolonging our own agony.

***

When you have two caring and supportive parents, who encourage you to think for yourself, who are stable and mature emotionally, mentally and spiritually, who exhibit all the qualities required in a loving relationship, you have an ideal set of parents.

A child of such parents would more than likely brim with confidence; his choice of mate as well as of friends would mirror those qualities of his parents; and his chances for making wise choices and planning a successful life would be great. Unfortunately, this is not the norm. Most people come from varying degrees of childhood trauma. Child sexual abuse is one of the most painful and exhibits certain behavior patterns—the individual common denominators.

Abuse victims behave and respond in ways that are different from children raised in an emotionally healthy environment. Survivors of childhood sexual abuse differ

from other people in two ways, which I have characterized as individual systems, and family systems. Family
systems, which we will discuss in a later chapter, show
the type of forest you lived in. For now, let's concentrate
on the individual ones, the trees.

These commonalities point to the origin of our unhappy lives. Once looked at, the picture becomes clearer.
It is difficult to believe that a person who had a prepon-
derance of these traits could live a happy life. Many of
them, especially the individual traits, are common to
anyone who suffered trauma in their childhood and
never healed from the pain. This is a list of identification,
not judgment. To help you with an honest appraisal, do
the following exercise. Check any that apply to you.

## Profile of a Childhood Sexual Abuse Victim

| Individual behavior patterns | |
|---|---|
| People-pleasing and rescuing at an early age | |
| Insomnia | |
| Excessive need to control | |
| Obsessive, compulsive behavior patterns | |
| Needy | |
| Low self-esteem | |
| Suicidal | |
| Weak boundaries | |
| Unhealthy choices in members of the opposite sex | |
| Neurotic tendencies | |
| Addictions: drugs, alcohol, sex, food, relationships | |
| Eating disorders | |
| Chronic illness | |
| Manic-depressive behavior (bipolar) | |
| Severe depression | |

In this chapter we're going to ask tough questions on the above, and then discuss each one. Some of these questions, while painful, are designed to encourage you to take an honest look at where your life has been in each area. Get a notebook and begin answering questions in as much detail as possible. As you follow the path of this program, you will discover that you are on a journey of enlightenment. The word literally means to be free from ignorance and misinformation. You received a lot of these in your early years and as you move through REPAIR, you will discard all of them. The Buddhist religion considers enlightenment as a final blessed state marked by the absence of suffering. This is what you are aiming for.

## People-Pleasing and Rescuing At an Early Age

Have you spent most of your life putting your own needs on hold while you take care of others? How does this feel? Do you resent it? Are you always the one who steps in first to rescue others from their dilemmas? Does adjusting your own behavior so that others will like you better sound like part of what you do? Do you need continual approval and find ways to get it even if it doesn't feel honest or the real you?

If you answered yes to any of these questions, how long have you been that way? Can you remember these traits starting shortly after you were sexually abused?

## Insomnia

How often do you get a good night's sleep? Do you use sleeping pills? Do you toss and turn and wake frequently once you do fall asleep? Do you feel exhausted upon waking and tired throughout the day? Do you suffer from nightmares?

Describe how your world would change if you got all the quality sleep you wanted every night of your life.

## Excessive Need to Control

Do you have an obsessive need to control those around you? Do you rant and rave about other people's lifestyles and behavior patterns and lecture them frequently about it? Do you feel that nothing in your universe can work well unless you handle it? Are you forever trying to tell other people how to live their lives? Are you the sort of person that others refer to as bossy?

Answer all of these questions honestly. Take a hard look at how much work it is to run other people's lives. Sometimes doing so is an unconscious choice we make to keep from looking at our own.

## Obsessive-Compulsive Behavior

Are you a fanatic about cleanliness and order? Do you have persistent, disturbing preoccupations? Are you opinionated or judgmental? Does the thought of change terrify you? Are you such a creature of habit that the slightest variation from your routine sends you into nail-biting frenzies?

Make a list of any of the above that describe you. Write next to each item what you'd like to change.

## Needy

Do you enjoy your own company? Do you find yourself phoning people frequently, then feeling embarrassed about it? Do you require other people in your life to distract you from sad times? Do you feel as if you pester friends and family with your problems? Do you need to interact with them in order to feel better about yourself? Are you comfortable about being alone?

## Low self-esteem

Who do you like best in the world? If the answer isn't you, you may want to write down why. Do you feel "less than," not worthy, inappropriate, unable to make decisions on your own? Do you make frequent apologies and excuses for why you do what you do? Do you find yourself looking up to almost everyone you know? Do you continually compare your life and yourself with others and feel wanting?

Make a list of all your character traits that you do not like.

Make a list of all your character traits that you do like.

Make a list of all the character traits you would like to have.

## Suicidal

Have you ever tried to take your own life? Do you wish you were dead? Do you often feel a sense of hopelessness and despair? Do you feel overwhelmed by your daily responsibilities? Does life seem meaningless and the world a dark and despairing place?

Describe the feelings that accompany these moments and what you think might have caused them, then write about how it would feel to let them go.

## Weak boundaries

Do you say yes when you mean no? Do you cringe after reacting without thinking? Do you find yourself spending time with people you don't care for and in situations with which you are uncomfortable? Do you make excuses to avoid certain people and certain choices you have made? Do you think things through before responding? Do you avoid overbearing, controlling people? How comfortable are you with saying NO? Do you have the courage of your own convictions or are you weak-kneed at the thought of defending them?

We all have the right to set and hold our own boundaries, those lines we draw that indicate our limits. When a child is sexually molested, this boundary has been violated. Since future abuse was more than likely set up at birth by the type of family systems they was born into, the kind of parents and grandparents they had, and environmental factors, the likelihood of their ability to create and hold boundaries is small. Even if a child had the ability to begin with, once sexually abused, setting her own boundaries becomes a frightening privilege. It requires assertiveness, a quality with which a victim of child sexual abuse has little familiarity; it requires confidence, another quality not common in victims; and especially it requires a high level of self-esteem that stems from not only knowing what rights they have, but believing these rights are inherently theirs. Low self-esteem is the core issue in all those who have been sexually abused as children.

Make a list of all activities coming up in the next week, as well as a list of all those people with whom you will be interacting. Then cross out all the things that you don't really want to do and the people you'd rather avoid. What is keeping you from having only the remaining ones on your list?

## Unhealthy Choices in Relationships

Does your significant other have a problem with alcohol or drugs? Is this person physically violent, emotionally unstable or controlling? Are there demands for sex, and abuse when if is denied? Is the relationship honest and fair minded? What is your partner's personal integrity like? How does this person treat children—ones common to you, or yours? What about parents? How does your spouse treat you? With respect? Consideration? Understanding? Is there honesty and mutual consideration in the relationship?

These are some of the questions you should ask yourself when you first begin a relationship. If the answers are not right, then neither is your choice. A future with anyone who doesn't rate the right answer to any of these questions is predictable. Most of us wait until we are in the depths of despair before we begin to notice the shortcomings of those with whom we have developed an emotional attachment. Since in a wounded child the heart is disconnected from the head, it is no wonder we choose someone who is unstable for our life's mate. People with low self-esteem generally pick partners who do not treat them well or are not of sound and noble character. It is difficult to see that you deserve the best when you do not believe you are the best. Foresight and good judgment, qualities denied to one who has been sexually abused as a child, are essential to our well-being. These qualities, among others, will be discussed in a later stage of this program.

Make a list of all the attributes you would like to have in a partner. Then ask yourself how many yours actually has. This will give you a good indication of whether your life will get better or worse. You will need to be ruthlessly honest and not build excuses. During this program, you will periodically do exercises where you will imagine the way you'd like your future to be. I cannot emphasize the importance of this enough. Your unconscious is taking notes. Nothing will be wasted. Picture a center in your mind where thousands of volunteers are running around organizing your responses, your thoughts, and your perceptions. Others are busy assembling them into bits and pieces of wisdom that emerge as your inner voices. As you progress through REPAIR, your inner voices will respond to their wake-up call and set in motion a solution for every problem in your life.

## Neurotic Tendencies

Do you feel as if others don't like you or are avoiding you? Do you find yourself having a distorted perception of reality? Do your friends and family accuse you of such? Are you unnecessarily anxiety-prone? Do you have phobias? Do you bite your nails? Shake with tremors? Have nervous tics or odd behavior patterns that stem from nervous disorders? Are you fearful of situations that most people take in their stride? Do you over-react to situations and wish you weren't so sensitive?

Make a list of any of the above and how you feel not only about having them, but where you think they might stem from, and how you would feel if they were not in your life.

## Addictions: Drugs, Alcohol, Sex, Relationships

Do you use prescription drugs or alcohol to excess? Do you smoke? Are you using any kind of illegal drugs? Do you feel anxiety-prone if you do not have frequent sex? Do you begin feeling insecure and anxious when not in the presence of your significant other? Do you modify your behavior and your choices to make your partner happy even when it is not what you really want? Do you feel you will die without your partner and/or are nothing without this person in your life?

When our life is one of despair, obsessing on anything that distracts us from the pain becomes paramount. We develop our own set of rules for survival. Whether they are healthy or not becomes a moot point. The more intense the addiction, whether it be drugs, alcohol, sex or relationships, the more it takes us away from our pain. We cannot see that we are prolonging it. You can only run for so long before reality settles in.

People who live healthy lives draw on the past for lessons to be learned and happy memories, and the future for goals for which they are striving; but they know how to relish the present. Childhood sexual abuse victims don't know how to live in present-time. It is always the despair and pain of the past and the wishful thinking of the future. Any present time awareness needs to be fogged over with an obsession or an addiction whether it be one with minor consequences such as obsessive talking or one of major consequences such as cocaine addiction. When they drag their baggage behind them, distract themselves with addictions, and live on fleeting hopes of being rescued, is it any wonder that one who was sexually molested sees their life as hopeless and themselves as helpless.

Make a list of any addictions in your life. Keep in mind that an addiction is anything that is a persistent compulsion, an activity meant to distract us from our own pain, characterized by an inability to relinquish it. Describe how you feel about each of these addictions,

Woman dragging baggage

what you get as a result of continuing to hook into them, and what you achieve if you no longer feel a craving for them.

## Eating disorders

Are you bulimic? Anorexic? Obese? Do you crave food when you are feeling emotional pain? Do you lie about your eating disorder and sneak food? Do you wear clothes on purpose that hide your bulk? Do you avoid mirrors?

Write a paragraph on any of these that fit you. Describe what it feels like to be bound by any eating disorder you have. How would you feel if they were not in your life?

## Chronic Illness

Do you suffer from chronic illness of any kind, either major or minor? How long have you had these? Did the onset of these disorders coincide with your childhood sexual abuse?

As the emotional pain of unresolved conflicts turns inward, it provides a ripe field for physical ailments. A long term relationship exits between childhood traumas and adult health status. They are linked together by a lifetime web of choices that create chronic illness. Smoking, overeating, alcohol and drug abuse, and unhealthy sexual behaviors are all coping mechanisms we use to make our way through a minefield of poor choices. As the stress this creates weakens the immune system, it produces cardiovascular problems, chronic obstructive pulmonary disorders, and digestive tract illnesses as well as muscular and head aches and pains. Even cancer is encouraged by this weakened immune system.

In the life of an untreated victim of child sexual abuse, these potentially life-threatening disorders worsen. One by one, our body systems begin to shut down. Even if we do not physically die, our joy in life dies. Since the human dimensions—spiritual, emotional, mental and physical—are all inter-related, once the joy is gone, it is only a matter of time before the body follows.

A treated victim not only has the blessings of being able to pass on to his children the results of his healthy behavior, but his body becomes the primary beneficiary. That victim, who is now a survivor, has a much greater chance to live to a ripe old age. The quality of those years improves dramatically as well. Think what this could mean for health care costs.

## Manic-Depressive Behavior (Bipolar)

Do you find yourself ecstatically happy one day and in the depths of despair the next? Do your emotions feel like they are on a roller coaster as you sky-rocket from one mood swing to another? Are you governed by what your feelings are at the moment, rather than working your way through life with logic and sensibility? Do you use your head before you use your words or do you use your words (and heart) before engaging your mind?

Extremes of emotional highs and lows in the victim are one of the most prominent repercussions of child sexual abuse. It becomes a way of life that in time feels normal. Isn't everybody high sometimes and low another? No. Healthy people, those who have never experienced childhood trauma, are emotionally stable. It doesn't mean they don't have joy in their life and it certainly doesn't mean sadness never visits. What it does mean is that these emotions don't reach roller-coaster peaks and valleys as a regular part of their life. On a day-to-day basis they are emotionally stable, keeping a steady course. Their responses to situations are coherent, reasonable and rational. They rarely, if ever, have unexplainable highs and then plunge into depression. They are firm in their resolutions and constant in their purpose. If their lives veer off course, they take whatever steps are necessary to restore equilibrium. A sexual abuse victim has little chance of achieving these character traits without recovery.

## Severe depression

Do you feel as if you live on the dark side of life, where happiness is elusive and a sense of peace and tranquility an unreachable goal? Do you feel heavy hearted and sad, a sense of loss and despair overcoming you on a frequent basis? Is it difficult for you to enjoy life? Does laughter elude you and has your sense of play disappeared? Does life seem not worth living?

An overwhelming feeling of hopelessness seems to fill the days of a person who was sexually abused as a child. There may be periodic distractions that bring temporary joy—the birth of a child, new furniture or a vacation, a new love in their life and so on—but the overall feeling is one of being unable to cope with whatever may come next. A sexually abused person doesn't wake in the morning excited about what the day may bring. They only hope it doesn't bring something they can't handle. A constant feeling of impending dread and an almost child-like desire for someone to rescue them colors their day; they're not sure from what, they only know that their burden weighs more than they can carry.

Many of the above qualities fall under the umbrella of co-dependency. Additional unhealthy behaviors that are also typical of a co-dependent are the following.

Do you make excuses for others when they hurt you? Do you put your needs last and those of others first, even when they don't deserve it? Do you find yourself unable to make the smallest decision without first checking it out with your partner? Do you buy expensive gifts even when you can't afford them? Do you say yes when you mean no? Later on when we look at our parents, you'll see how much we imitate their dysfunction with these unhealthy behaviors.

List any of these qualities that describe you. Write about how it feels to have these behavior patterns in your life.

***

We all have some of the aforementioned qualities. When we have too many or they cause distress or despair, they are symptoms of deeper problems, usually stemming from our childhood. Sexual abuse is often the culprit. The number of childhood traumas that have their roots in sexual abuse is much larger than people realize. There is nothing quite like shame of our own bodies and what was done to them to create lives filled with despair and cause us to want to hide that most secret part of ourselves.

Taught from childhood that giving till it hurts and turning the other cheek are commendable qualities, we adopt the behavior of codependents to hide our shame. Many of us convince ourselves that codependency is noble. For example: the wife of an alcoholic makes excuses for why she can't take the children and leave. What would he do without her? She programs herself into believing she is doing the right thing.

When we choose a partner who has already shown signs of contributing nothing but grief, we say we are in love and can't possibly leave. Thinking ahead to the stage when we are no longer in love but in fact are drowning in reality is something we never learned and we don't want to learn when we're in that hazy glow that becomes an addiction.

When our weight creeps beyond what is healthy and heads for obesity, we blame it on Mom's admonishment to eat everything on our plate because the children in China are starving. We buy larger clothes to hide the added weight. We hang around with people who weigh more than we do so we won't look so bad. We watch a lot of television so we won't have to think about it. We tell ourselves we'll go on a diet tomorrow, or crack jokes about the See Food diet we're on. We enhance our sense of humor to hide further. Doesn't everybody love a clown? They won't notice our low self-esteem if we keep them laughing.

Perhaps being overweight makes us feel empowered. Surely no one will tangle with us when we are big. When we lose weight because of a diet, we also start getting into fear again. It is a false sense of protection. Being big has nothing to do with whether or not you'll be able to protect yourself.

When promiscuity becomes a way of life and we sleep with a married man, we tell ourselves, with a certain dark humor, that the commandment *Thou shalt not covet thy neighbor's wife,* doesn't mean coveting the husband, only the wife. After all, he's the one committing adultery, not us.

Denial goes on and on.

When we see others making healthy choices, walking away from abuse, and taking strong steps to change their lives, we see them as selfish, perhaps even arrogant. When a friend tells us that she is not going to date so and so because he's not good enough for her, we're embarrassed for her large ego. Never mind that he stood her up twice in a row and that his idea of a great date is to show up with his dirty laundry and a bag from McDonald's.

Sometimes, after finding out about our mate's own dysfunctional childhood, we make excuses for him. "How awful that his father hung him from a tree in a gunny sack all day when he was a small boy. No wonder he's always angry." We forget that we too came from a place of dysfunction and yet we never became abusive. Or maybe we did. Childhood pain is never an excuse for molesting or hurting others once we grow up.

A lot of this was programmed into us as children. What our parents learned, they taught us; what we learn, we pass on to our children. The vicious cycle travels from one generation to another. Like a contagious disease, it impacts every member of the family. A child who was sexually abused is not the only wounded family member. It has been said that witnesses to incest suffer even more than the actual victim. The sister that escaped rape because she lay in an upper bunk grows up, not only feeling guilty for having escaped, but hypervigilant and terrified of trusting anyone. The brother who couldn't step in and help feels guilt as does the mother who stands by and watches. The grandparents who see, but don't understand, feel helplessness, which in turn damages their self-esteem. In a wounded family, no one emerges unscathed.

As so eloquently explained in *John Bradshaw on The Family Systems*, each family member has an impact on the other—for good and for bad. The results are so far-reaching that years later that same family gathering for a reunion immediately slips into the unhealthy dynamics originally created in the early family system. The results of child sexual abuse and incest are a downward spiral created through a lifetime of problems and disorders. It takes only one to break the cycle.

For some, hitting what Twelve Step Programs refer to as their "bottom," may be the only way to recognize that their life is not working. Further signs that occur at this stage are a deepening of despair and flashbacks. Thoughts of death, of throwing yourself in front of a moving truck, chain smoking as you eat foods heavily laden with fat, dressing slovenly and refusing to follow basic good grooming rules, constant negativity and frequent crying spells followed by periods of despondency, are all part of the pattern of a child sexual abuse victim heading toward his bottom.

If flashbacks happen, they can be terrifying. Where did that picture in your mind come from? A bedroom door half open has your heart racing with terror and a shadowed picture accelerating in your brain. Why does gray hair and age spots make you suddenly think of your lecherous great-uncle and bring nausea and dizziness? Why does the mention of the book *Lolita* paralyze you with fear? When another in a series of therapists asks if you've ever been molested, why, when your answer is no, do you feel you'd just told a lie? Articles in newspapers about incest and sexual abuse of children cause you to begin trembling and head for the bathroom to vomit.

One of the most frequently asked questions in child sexual abuse recovery is remembering, and the role it plays. Some of us remember with searing pictures. Usually, those who experience this learn to retreat behind a mask of emotional detachment. The ones whose memories lurk in shadowed pictures are generally more overtly troubled, more emotionally unstable, their despairing natures more visible to the outside world. Remembering is not important, but it helps to validate what was.

The lack of remembering does not in any way signify a lack of sexual abuse. If Dad lies in bed in an alcoholic stupor, reeking of vodka and slurring his words but you never saw him take a drink and there are no empty bottles nearby, would you say he was drunk? If you came home and Dad was in a raging mood, Mom had a blackened eye and was shaking with tremors every time she looked at him, would you think he might have hit her, especially if he had a history of such a behavior pattern?

So, if you remember a nightmare from your childhood where a steamroller was coming over you, if you require large amounts of sex to feel worthy, (or can't bear to be touched) if you have been date-raped or if you are living with an abusive mate, why would you not think that you had been violated as a child? If you add to this picture a family history that contains a womanizing grandfather, a sexually promiscuous father, and a co-dependent mother, all in a patriarchal family, your evidence mounts at an alarming rate.

By now you should have a clear picture of what a victim of child sexual abuse looks like. You should also know if you fit in that picture. If you are still uncertain or feel that even if it does apply to you, it happened long ago and has no impact on your life today, then take a closer look. As we said in the beginning, if you are joyful and in a healthy relationship, working in a positive manner toward achieving what you want, have only positive and uplifting people in your life, and have no screaming child inside of you, filled with trauma and pain, then this program is obviously not what you need. Perhaps curling up with a current bestseller and a bowl of popcorn is more appropriate.

Many victims, sexually abused as children but not by a family member, fail to see that it is as traumatic as incest. In truth, they are one and the same. The definition of the word incest in the dictionary may relate only to blood relatives, but as we clearly described earlier, anyone in a position of power that violates us sexually creates the same world of despair. We are talking about the direct and anguishing results of a childhood trauma relating to sex. When it is a family member, especially a parent, the violation of trust and the betrayal by one who we expected to keep us safe can be more deeply ingrained and difficult to work through. That does not negate the pain of being molested by someone other than a family member. Children do not have the mental maturity to differentiate between those non-family members who abuse power for their own purposes and family members who we thought had our well-being in mind. The betrayal is the same in both cases and this program can heal the one as well as the other.

Sometimes, behavior patterns that are the result of our incest or other child sexual abuse are the very ones we need to eradicate in order to be happy. They keep us from making an honest appraisal of our life. Twelve Step

programs talk about being "brutally honest." It is a necessary ingredient in working this program. Leftovers of
sexual abuse can keep us from *recognizing* what our life
has become and hold us back from taking the first step
onto the bridge. These include listening to destructive
messages from our childhood rather than arriving at our
own conclusions; clinging to old ways because they are
familiar—no matter how painful—instead of accepting
change; and lacking faith in our own ability.

## Recognizing the duplication of relationships from our childhood

Victims of childhood sexual abuse often re-enact a
script from their growing-up years, hoping this time it
will turn out differently. As adults, they find themselves
drawn to members of the opposite sex who have similar
qualities to their perpetrators. This is almost always
done at an unconscious level.

The reasons are complex. We had a love/hate relationship with the perpetrator and when we never
achieved a healthy bonding with them as children, that
need went unsatisfied. As adults, we look for satisfaction
in the face of every potential partner. Many a victim of
sexual abuse grew up saying they would never marry
anyone like their father, and yet they continued to do so
over and over.

We needed someone who could fill the empty hole inside ourselves and as adults find, sometimes in almost
exact replication, the dual nature of our original family.
On the outside, charming, bright, enlightened... on the
inside... seething sexual abuse and manipulative, controlling qualities.

Most of the time, people in a position of power appear all-knowing, and all-powerful, therefore worthy of being someone with whom we wish to spend the rest of our lives. The truth is that because of low self-esteem, our unconscious mind feels unworthy of a partner who is healthy, so we place the dysfunctional one we chose on a pedestal. This blinds us to their true nature and re-creates our own misery as a wounded child.

Recovery can become the ointment we place on our wounds. Without the right program, the ointment may not help. When floundering through recovery without proper direction, you run the risk of prolonging the time by joining unhealthy groups, choosing a therapist who knows nothing about recovery from child sexual abuse, or getting sidetracked by reading books that have little to do with healing from the abuse.

Let's get you started on that first step across the bridge. Now that you have recognized the origin of your problems, you are ready for the second stage of REPAIR.

| 4 | Entry |  |
|---|---|---|

**New beginnings are always difficult,**
**But they are the only solution**
**To moving forward with your life.**

*For without change, we die, locked in the same prison.*

A pattern seems to precede entry into recovery. After being molested, as we grow older our life starts to fall apart, a process so gradual that we may not be aware of it. One failed relationship leads to another. What started out as partying becomes alcoholism, and we suffer lack of confidence despite getting older. Making wise choices eludes us and we begin to realize that our life presents little joy, that some of our choices add to our plummeting self-esteem.

We're not sure who or what to blame. We thought life would get better as we got older. If only this or that would happen, all would be well. But it never does and we never get well. Our despair deepens and hope dies. Bad experiences based on unhealthy choices pile up in closets in our mind with doors we won't open. We are hardly aware that those closets contain childhood trauma from our sexual abuse and that we have been trained early on to keep them under lock and key.

Cynicism, low grade depression and anger begin. It's so insidious that we scarcely notice. Then one day we wake up and realize that life is going too fast and it's not turning out the way we wanted. We run out of places and ways to hide. The closets in our mind fill to capacity and we can no longer hold back the dam. We are ripe for entry into recovery.

As I said before, we usually arrive at this place in our forties, although for some, it happens much earlier. It depends on our tolerance for pain as well as how close we are to our "bottom." I've mentioned the term "bottom" previously. It is an interesting term, coined by Twelve Steppers and literally means the lowest point. We don't reach this overnight.

Having a high tolerance for pain can keep us out of recovery for years. That very tolerance is why we remain in relationships that don't work. During the passage of time we heap trauma upon trauma, incorporating more unhealthy behavior patterns into our lives, and losing precious time that could have been joyous. From childhood on, we continuously readjusted to unsatisfactory situations instead of walking away from them. No wonder the abuse grew as our tolerance increased.

While going through REPAIR, you will discover as you learn to set boundaries that your tolerance for pain will decrease. Abuse aimed in your direction that you used to grit your teeth over will no longer be acceptable. You will start seeing with great clarity not only who the good guys and the bad guys are, but what is appropriate behavior and what isn't. Once completing REPAIR, you will get used to people asking why you've become so intolerant. Those will be the voices of others who have not yet learned to set realistic levels of tolerance. It is one thing to be patient in a grocery line, and quite another to put up with a vicious verbal attack from a co-worker, enabling them to continue their bad behavior.

A frequently asked question is, "Why do some who suffer the most severe of traumas deal well with the repercussions and others who seemed to have minimal abuse grow up with more painful adult years?" The degree of what happened to us is not always proportionate to the degree of our fate. Many factors play a part. A child who had a loving and supportive mother may find it easier to overcome the incest damage from her father. Another, whose incest trauma was relatively minor but who also had an abusive mother and other heinous environmental factors, may find herself a drug addict and prostitute at an early age. The total picture needs to be seen. But in all pictures, sexual abuse and its resultant shame are still the core issues.

Sometimes it is easier for us to look at a much milder trauma as the focal point for why our lives are scarred. Remembering the pain of not getting a hoped for bicycle at Christmas or a cruel taunt of a schoolmate is much easier to deal with than the real reason we are suffering. Opening the closet that contains a sexual abuse perpetrator and the slaughter of our own innocence is not something we are so willing to look at. Many of us approach recovery in stages. We gain courage as we gradually work up to the real culprit. Do not despair if you open only the less traumatic closets first. In time, every closet will be opened.

Entering recovery occurs in various ways. The most prominent are:

## Individual Therapy

This sometimes begins at the urging of a family physician, a spiritual advisor, or a family member who can no longer bear to watch you suffer. Shop for a therapist as you would for any major purchase: ask questions, request references etc. Not all therapists are created equal. Check their credentials; interview them. Have they ever worked with a patient on childhood sexual abuse issues?

Have they themselves or any family member ever experienced incest? How long have they been practicing? What is their success rate in bringing clients through recovery? Do they have additional tools to suggest to help you on your journey? Brainstorm other questions so you will be prepared when you go to your first appointment.

Some therapists are not qualified to deal with such a sensitive and painful issue as incest. Keep in mind that, while a guided tour is optimum, it is always possible to find your way along the bridge without a guide. You are never really alone. Additional help is available. If that help is chosen carefully and utilized to its fullest, you can complete the program without a therapist.

## Group Therapy and Programs

Twelve Step Programs, i.e., Codependents Anonymous, Incest Survivors Anonymous, Adult Children of Alcoholics, Alcoholics Anonymous and others, as well as incest recovery groups in local churches, domestic violence groups, etc. all prove to be not only invaluable help, but almost a necessity in finding your way across the bridge. We will discuss them in greater length during the Process part of this program. They provide the maps you will need to complete your journey. Sometimes working hand in hand with more than one is a good idea. Here, common sense enters the picture.

If you join a group that is non-supportive of your goals, is not all embracing of your problems, and does not use personal integrity as their guideline, they are not right for you. If they prove interesting but of little help, continue your search for another group, one that will help you to move across that bridge.

This includes Twelve Step Programs as well as others. Just because you are uncomfortable with one Twelve Step group doesn't mean it is the fault of the group. Perhaps the participants are not quite tailored to the kind of support you need. Just as all therapists are not alike, not all groups are alike. Unfortunately, some recovery groups have adopted destructive behavior with excessive control and power plays. They can sabotage progress and prey on a victim's vulnerability. It is up to you to pay attention to your inner voices; that intuitive part of you. It will never lie. If you feel that a group is not right, it probably isn't. But don't make a snap judgment. As with Twelve Step Programs, give each group six sessions. If you still feel uncomfortable, it is time to search for another. Keep in mind that every time you expose yourself to other people's dysfunctions, you run the risk of creating more of your own. You don't need something like that to slow your progress in getting healthy.

For those not familiar with the Twelve Steps, they are listed on page 58 and again in the Resource section at the back of this book.

***

## The Twelve Steps

1.  We admitted we were powerless over others and that our lives had become unmanageable.

2.  We came to believe that a power greater than ourselves could restore us to sanity.

3.  We made a decision to turn our lives over to the care of God as we understood God.

4.  We made a fearless and searching moral inventory of ourselves.

5.  We admitted to God, to ourselves, and to another human being the exact nature of our wrongs.

6.  We were entirely ready to have God remove all these defects of character.

7.  We humbly asked God to remove our shortcomings.

8.  We made a list of people we had harmed and became willing to make amends to them all.

9.  We made direct amends wherever possible, except when to do so would harm them or others.

10. We continued to take personal inventory and when we were wrong, promptly admitted it.

11. We sought through prayer and meditation to improve our conscious contact with God, praying only for knowledge of His will and the power to carry it out.

12. Having had a spiritual awakening as a result of these steps, we tried to carry this message to others and to practice these principles in all our affairs.

## A Combination of Both

When you utilize the services of both, the qualified therapist will be your primary guide and the Twelve Steps and other programs part of the path you take. There will be times when a one-on-one and cross-talk—a style not followed in most Twelve Step programs—is what you need at the moment. Keep in mind that people in programs, while they too are on a journey of healing, do not necessarily have the expertise that a therapist can provide. For those sensitive moments when you require privacy and wisdom that may not be available from the lay person, a trained therapist is your best bet. If this is beyond your budget, check your medical insurance policy. Often there are hidden benefits that cover post-traumatic stress.

## Supportive and Non-Supportive Family Members and Friends

One of the most important needs you will have is the circle of friends and family who make up your support group. Not everyone will be on this list. Your nuclear family may not want to dredge up old family stuff. Worse yet, they may not believe you and may ridicule your efforts. Anyone who does not take your recovery seriously has no place in your inner circle. Mom may not want to desecrate Dad's image. In patriarchal families, keeping Dad on his pedestal is mandatory. Secrecy is the biggest reason incest is epidemic. Why would you want to protect someone who has physically violated you? Why would you want to include in your support group someone who encourages you to protect that person?

Eliminate those who might hinder your progress. Emphasize that you are on a journey and that arriving at

the end is the only thing that matters. Keep only supportive people in your life. Any attempts to sabotage your
recovery will keep you from reaching the end of that
bridge.

Seek those willing to listen, those who genuinely care
and encourage you. You will be surprised at how many
who touch your life will soon be touched by yours. Often,
during recovery you meet kindred spirits who, if it were
not for your courageous efforts in coming out of hiding,
would not be able to face their own childhood traumas.
The sad truth is that more people have been traumatized
by sexual abuse, either to themselves or to a loved one,
than have not.

As we have already learned, the trauma of a victim of
child sexual abuse has an impact on all family members.
Two healthy people have a great chance of finding happiness in a relationship. One healthy and one not so
healthy have a more difficult chance, and two unhealthy
people stand very little chance of having a happy life together. That is not to say that once one begins the
journey, the other will not follow, but do not enter recovery with this as your goal. Your primary purpose is
getting yourself healthy, not your partner. If something
beyond that happens, it will be an added blessing.

Many of us enter recovery while living with an abuser.
A variety of responses occur, not always to our liking.
They may be supportive at first—a pleasant surprise.
Beware and be patient. If the support is not genuine,
their real motives will surface quickly. Often, changing
our own behavior through recovery prompts our mate to
begin to change. But it is not something to count on.

What may happen instead is that they find new ways
to manipulate, thus discouraging you from committing

to your program. Adopt a feeling of detachment. There is no way you can convince abusers that what you are doing is not only vital for you, but could ultimately be best for them. They won't listen. Refuse to cooperative with any maneuvers they employ to distract you. If their abuse accelerates, find a support group in your area for battered women. Don't let the title mislead you. Battered does not only apply to physical abuse. Battered women's support groups and women's shelters are familiar with the cycle of violence that begins with emotional threats, then swiftly leads to economic abuse, isolation, emotional abuse, patriarchal power plays and using the children as weapons. It is all about power and control, the twin demons that set you up to be molested in the first place.

Keep in mind that as you cross that bridge, you will begin to see your mate—if he is an abuser—in a different light. Power plays, manipulations and controls will be more obvious and you will be less willing to buy into them. As you begin to set boundaries, they may retaliate by accelerating their own unhealthy behavior. This is no time for a faint heart. If separation from an abuser gives you the courage to work through your own recovery without faltering, that may well be the choice you have to make.

If friends or family harass you to split up from an abuser before you are ready, your despair will deepen. You never walk alone until your legs are strong enough to hold you. Let those who care know what you are going through and that all changes have to be done in your time frame, not theirs. When you are ready, although it may still be painful to go through a separation, you will have the strength to walk through it. If your loved ones choose to abandon you because they can't bear your pain, that is their decision. If the bond is strong enough, this will not happen. And if it does, they may return when you have completed recovery.

Codependents are hampered in their progress by focusing on their mate's needs rather than their own. It is extremely difficult to pull away from this trait. Keep in mind that as you build strength by working through RE-PAIR, in time it will be easier. While crossing this bridge, it is imperative that you put your progress in the program above all other needs. If your mate, abusive or not, can not be supportive of this, you may eventually decide to go it alone.

A word here about those fortunate enough to have a supportive mate. It can be hard on them to help you work through recovery. They may be confused. As you begin going through the recovery process, some things will be difficult for them to understand. Certain facets to your relationship may be put on hold. This adds to your mate's confusion. Using clear communication to keep them posted on your progress will enable them to be supportive of your journey. They may not always understand what you are going through, but letting them know it will improve not only your own life but the relationship the two of you are building. This will go a long way toward enlisting their support. Twelve Steps Programs are available to them as well. Encourage them to attend. Working a Twelve Step program is always an improvement in anyone's life.

It is not a good idea to attend Twelve Step meetings together. This can serve to inhibit both of you as well as create enormous conflicts once you leave the meeting. Many a couple has gone their separate ways because one or the other was dismayed at their partner's revelations at a meeting regarding disputes in their private lives. If you go to a meeting alone, while there you may arrive at the appropriate way to approach your mate on an issue that has long been churning, but blurting it out while he or she is sitting next to you is an almost guaranteed way to sabotage accomplishment. The Twelve Steps were founded on anonymity and as such, all participants are bound by their word to not repeat anything they hear. This makes it a safe place. Twelve Steppers new to the program are fragile and it takes all their courage to keep going in recovery. They don't need more conflict in their personal life.

***

Our point of entry may occur when we reach our bottom. Everyone's is different. It may be the fifth drunk driving charge, finding out you have just tested HIV positive after being promiscuous for many years, winding up in the Emergency Room from a failed suicide attempt, a child or spouse saying they can no longer bear being around you, or the timely realization of your own acute misery. Sadly, the bottom for some is death.

Sometimes, no one urges us. A word or phrase heard on a talk show, a movie or TV program that bears an eerie resemblance to our own life, can be the spur that sends us into a program. In the beginning, even the word *recovery* is foreign, as if it belongs to someone we've read about in a magazine but has no bearing as an answer to our own tormented life. Whatever it may be, keep following whatever thread leads you onto that first step.

## Commitment

There is little purpose in entering recovery without commitment. Many incest victims, having heard it is the answer to their prayers, race off to a local Codependent Meeting. They wander out two hours later, scratching their head. *Who wants to listen to other people's problems? I'm trying to get away from them,* or *everyone in there looked like a loser. My life isn't that bad.* Sound familiar?

Rather than focusing on what you see, listen to what you hear at the meeting. You may see a room full of troubled people, but what you are hearing is a room full of courage. The saying in Twelve Step programs that you must attend at least six meetings has a lot of validity. Something magical happens by then. You start to get it. The feeling that you are in the right place overwhelms you as you begin to identify with their stories. Only a sense of commitment will carry you through those meetings. Anyone who survived years of living with abuse can certainly survive six meetings at Twelve Steps. In time, you'll wonder how you ever got along without them.

Only one person can turn your life around—you. No one can travel the journey for you. Friends may be supportive of your efforts. They may applaud your progress. But in the dark of night in the middle of that bridge, when you look down at the deep waters and want to turn back, your sense of commitment will keep you moving forward. You must find a secret place inside of you to bond with and make a pact with. You must promise not to falter or run.

If you knew for certain that going across that bridge would change your life dramatically to a place where life became everything you wanted, would you turn back? Of course you wouldn't. While there will be times during your journey when recovery may be painful, times when the load seems too heavy to bear, you must separate yourself from those fears. Nothing could be as bad as what's behind you. Lean into the wind and feel the presence of something happening in your life greater than anything you could have predicted. You are in the process of becoming all you were meant to be. That is an awesome promise.

Keep in mind that everyone's timetable for crossing that bridge is different. Many factors come in to play. Only you will know when it is time to enter the next step in your program. Only you will know when it is time to confront your abusers or even the manner in which to do so. Recovery is very individual. One person may take five years; their reasons don't define you. If another has already arrived at the end of the bridge and you are still floundering at the beginning, don't give up. Often, quantum leaps occur at unexpected moments that will propel you forward at a speed you couldn't have predicted.

Everything you are learning takes time to process. Parts of it will feel comfortable, even exciting. Interviewing cooperative family members to construct your history can not only prove enlightening, but entertaining. Other tasks may not feel as comfortable. Always keep in mind that while you move across that bridge, you will be building strengths that, in the beginning, you could not have predicted. As in building a house, the foundation will be strong enough so that when you get ready to place the roof, it will seem like an easy task.

## Preparing For Your Journey

As with all journeys you must prepare before you begin to cross that bridge. Your preparations should include plenty of sleep, quiet time alone for daily meditation and a healthy diet that follows the basic food groups, especially plenty of fresh fruits and vegetables. Eating well means feeling well. If you don't believe this, spend one week eating only junk food and the next eating healthy food. You are in a healing mode, not only emotionally, mentally and spiritually, but physically.

Keep your fluid intake high, drinking at least eight glasses of water a day. Surround yourself with pleasant and healthy activities, and set aside a part of each day for exercise. One of the best is walking. If you have a park or a scenic setting nearby, combine a daily walk with meditation. Having that physical side of you in a good place will go a long way toward promoting total wellness and will do wonders for your emotional stability.

Check with your local health food store. A number of herbs have a calming effect. Chamomile and other herb teas aid sleep disorders. Evening Primrose Oil, available at any drug store, is a great natural way to promote emotional stability. Avoid cigarettes, alcohol and excessive sweets. Alcohol is a depressant, and a thirty-minute walk will do you more good than a few beers. Although studies are emerging regarding the benefit of a daily glass of wine in warding off cardiovascular health disorders, use your head and remember, moderation in all things. Follow these rules for good sleep:

1.  Keep caffeine intake to a minimum.
2.  Use salt sparingly, if at all.

3. A hot bath with a good book, soft music, and a lighted candle (white for serenity) has a calming effect before bedtime.

4. Eat early in the evening and avoid large meals if possible.

5. Always retire at the same time.

6. Establish a comforting and stabilizing ritual prior to bedtime, i.e., lay out clothes for the next day, brush your teeth and bathe, set the clock, read something bland for a few minutes before turning the light out.

7. Avoid intense or worrisome phone calls before retiring, as well as any late-night dealings that may encourage stress (paying bills right before bedtime will usually ensure tossing and turning).

8. Don't exercise to excess in the evening—a short walk perhaps to ease tensions. Keep in mind that daily exercise improves sleep.

9. Make sure the room temperature is comfortable.

10. If you begin to toss and turn, get out of bed and fix a glass of warm milk or non-caffeine herbal tea. Insomnia intensifies once you begin worrying about it, so anything you can do to distract yourself eliminates the problem.

Maintaining these simple rules will ease the discomfort of your journey. While the symbolic bridge you're on may sway, and the waters below may look dark and scary, you need only utilize the suggestions in this program to find the courage to keep going.

As I said earlier, new beginnings are always hard. We prefer the predictable, the timeworn regime. Our life may be miserable, but it's ours and it's familiar. Following the

program REPAIR will require change, and change is difficult. But change is what brought your life into a place of
darkness, and change will serve as the tool to take you
into the light. No one escapes change, a constant in life.
So, since it is inevitable that you must face it, wouldn't
you prefer that which will bring good? Keep these truths
in mind as you approach the next stage of our program.

In the coming pages, you will find many exercises
that at first may seem overwhelming. Do all of them in
your own time. None are designed to be done overnight.
They may require much thought and the proper moment
to approach them. Or perhaps you'll want to do them
more than once. There are no rules except to follow the
stages. Put this book aside and work on another part of
the program, perhaps attending Twelve Step meetings, if
you are not yet comfortable with them. Keep in mind
that they are all tools to encourage you to begin thinking
about the stages you will be going through. Words have
power, and the more words you write in these exercises
at the moments when they are called upon to put in an
appearance, the stronger you'll feel.

I can promise that if you follow through on a pact to
stay on the bridge, the rewards will be overwhelming. As
you come closer to the end of that bridge, you will see
wonderful things waiting on the other side. You'll develop
a sense of well-being. You may find yourself singing and
smiling more, as if you know something others don't.
You do. Plans will begin to formulate in your head about
what to do with the rest of your life. It will all be hazy at
first, but little by little, everything will become clear.
Keep this in mind as you progress to the next phase of
REPAIR.

| **5** | **Process** |  |
|---|---|---|

*Do whatever works—*

*And everything else will fall into line.*

Earlier, I mentioned building a house. When you do so you start with the basement or a foundation. From there the walls take shape, giving you a frame. Soon the roof goes on and windows and doors follow. If you want the house to last for many years, you need the right tools and quality materials. Shoddy workmanship, cheap materials, inaccurate building instructions, and especially a poor choice for a site, will cause your dream home to become a nightmare as it falls apart. This should come as no surprise.

In many ways, the life of an incest victim is much like a house that was poorly built. Parents who are ill-equipped themselves can hardly raise healthy, vibrant children. Unhealthy messages are inevitable from those who are in charge of creating our personalities, our temperaments, and our way of making choices. Victims of child sexual abuse need to rebuild their *own* home.

The right tools are important. They will include the following.

## Recovery Books and CDs

The market is flooded with recovery books and CDs. Every conceivable mental and emotional aberration known to man has been researched and written about. Child sexual abuse is no exception. Avail yourself of both the library and your local book store to search for those with which you are not only the most comfortable but those that provide insight and support for your particular need. Reading these books will give you additional knowledge and deepen your understanding of what happens to a molested person and why. You are embarking on a journey of education as well as healing. No education is complete without books.

CDs or tapes are especially invaluable tools for getting well. There are a number of ways to listen to them: while you are driving, while you clean the house or do yard work, using an iPod on your morning hike, playing them at night while you soak in a hot bubble bath. These words will become a part of your vocabulary and will change your way of thinking, so it is vital that you recognize them as truth. Keep in mind that the key is not only listening, but hearing. Reinforcement comes through repetition. That's why it is so important to listen frequently to the recordings. John Bradshaw's *Healing the Shame That Binds You* is one of the most beneficial. At the back of this book is a resource guide with suggestions for recovery and post-recovery books and recordings.

## The Bridge

The Bridge of Recovery, a visualization tool, is a vital part of REPAIR. Look at the illustration on p. 21 frequently and use it as a source for imagery. If you were going on a trip to Europe, you would no doubt think often of the wonderful sights you were going to see. You would count the days until you experienced the pleasure. You wouldn't be worrying about how much the trip will cost, for fear that you would change your mind. You would only think about the importance of your destination. The Bridge represents the journey you will take, and what lies on the other side represents your destination. What lies on this side is what will continue to happen in your life if you don't begin. The most important part of a journey is the first step. After that, you need only keep on moving. Do the following exercises before you enter this Bridge. (As with all the exercises in this book, if you are more comfortable with it and need the extra room, write your answers on a separate piece of paper.)

## What Waits Behind Me If I Don't Enter The Bridge?

(Examples: shame, alcoholism, promiscuity, eating disorders, suicide, despair, health problems, unhappiness, poor choices, co-dependent behavior patterns, etc.).

Describe vividly each of these that are prevalent in your life as well as any others you can think of.

_____

_____

_____

_____

_____

## Fears you will encounter as you cross the bridge, and solutions to combat them

(Examples: Problem—I'll feel too alone. Solution—I'll build a strong support group among friends, family and groups and utilize them whenever I feel this way. Problem—Looking at the pain of what happened is too overwhelming. Better the devil I know than the devil I don't. Solution—I'll check my list of all the things waiting for me at the end of the bridge, then compare it to the list behind me. My choice will be easier after that.)

Write your own list and possible solutions

| Problem | Solution |
|---------|----------|
|         |          |
|         |          |
|         |          |
|         | .        |
|         |          |

Keep in mind that inside each of us lies an untapped well of strength. We must be strong enough to cross the bridge; we have already survived so much.

## What lies on the other side of the bridge, waiting for me?

(Examples: joy, strong self-esteem, healthy choices, honesty, peace, a feeling of being centered and capable, fulfillment, problem resolution oriented, serenity, etc.).

As you write, picture each of these to their fullest. They will act as a beacon guiding you across the bridge and one day will be a part of your life.

_____

_____

_____

_____

_____

Now, picture yourself entering the bridge. Like all journeys, you want this one to be successful. It is the most important one you will ever take. Crossing this bridge will bring you to a world beyond your wildest expectations. Reread the lists you have just written at least once a day to reinforce the purpose of your journey.

## Construct a Magic Mirror

This may be the most significant thing you do as you cross that bridge. Your Magic Mirror will become your new parents. When you were a child, inevitably you received a lot of messages, some of which were unhealthy. *Don't touch yourself there. Bad girl. You're always lying about everything. I knew you were going to turn out like your father—no good. I'll tell you what you like and don't like. You're lazy.* And so on. Unfortunately, there were probably more negative messages than positive. Your brain is stuffed with them and what's worse, you no doubt believe them. It takes tremendous force for an adult to withstand these "not okay" messages, much less for a child.

You will need to get rid of every one. But it is not enough to rid yourself of these damaging messages. You need to replace them with healthy ones. Make a list of all the unhealthy messages you can remember, no matter how small or how early they were given. Even if the one giving the message convinced you they were true—but you know differently—write them down. Read over the list of unhealthy messages you received as a child and rewrite them the way you would like. Below is an example of what your list might look like.

| Unhealthy message | Healthy replacement message |
|---|---|
| You never do anything I tell you. | I choose to do what I think is right. |
| You're stupid. You can't even get an A in English. | I'm very bright and can get an A in anything I choose. |
| Your room is a pigsty. It shows what your mind is like. | I'm a creative person and that's what happens when your mind is full of creative ideas. |

Write some of your own.

| Unhealthy message | Healthy replacement message |
|---|---|
| | |
| | |
| | |
| | |
| | |

Next, you will need to gather affirmations for your Magic Mirror. Select any from the lists below that resonate with you. If you feel a strong emotional reaction to the affirmation, that is an indication you might have an issue around that. The following are some suggestions.

**Healing**

- No wound heals overnight, but little by little.
- As my heart heals, I will learn to love in exciting, powerful new ways.
- My maturity level will grow in proportion to the amount of pain I put behind me, and the wisdom I acquire as I move through the stages of REPAIR.

**Courage**

- The only antidote for fear is courage.
- I will trust that all is well, in spite of any fears I have.
- An unknown fear is better than a familiar pain.

- Whatever I fear grows in proportion to my obsession with it.

- I can get through dark situations. I only need to go as far as I can see. By the time I get there, I'll be able to see further.

- We all have monsters. Maybe it's fear of new situations. Maybe it's jealousy. The more attention I give the monsters, the more powerful they become.

## Overcoming Problems

- A mistake is something I do; it's not who I am.

- There is no problem too difficult to handle with all the help available to me.

- All the problems are in my head. So are the solutions.

- Unfinished business doesn't go away.

- The only thing that's really the end of the world is the end of the world.

## Anger

- I have a right to feel anger, and a responsibility to deal appropriately with my anger.

- I may need to get angry to set a limit, but I don't need to stay angry to enforce it.

## Pain

- Recovery does not mean freedom from pain. Recovery means learning to take care of myself when I'm in pain.

- I can stop my pain and get control of my life.

- Pain is inevitable; suffering is optional. - Kathleen Casey

- I will accept pain and disappointment as part of life.

- If sorrow or pain enters my life, I can lean into it and become stronger.

## Change

- I'm the only one who can change my life.
- The more choices I make, the more alive I feel. The more alive I feel, the healthier my choices.
- I am capable of making my most important decisions.
- Losing my freedom of choice is a bitter pill to swallow.
- There is no way to avoid changes in life, so why not make them positive ones?
- I will give up regrets about the past and fears about the future. I will make the most of this day.
- Healthy choices are all around. I can learn to make them.

## Attitude

- "As we think, so we are." My mind works powerfully for my good, and just as powerfully to my detriment when I allow fear to intrude on my thoughts.
- A change of attitude is all I need to move from where I am to a better place.
- I need to believe that I deserve the best life has to offer. If I don't believe that, I need to change what I believe.
- If I always do what I've always done, I'll always get what I've always had.

## Negativity

- I will avoid negative people.
- I can learn to let go of negative energy.

- If someone else has a bad day, it doesn't necessarily have anything to do with me.
- I don't have to believe lies.

## Relationships

- I can recognize the difference between relationships that work and those that don't.
- Boundaries are worth every bit of time and energy it takes to set and enforce them. They will provide me with more time and energy.
- Friends are a joy. Today, I will reach out to my friends.
- If I think I'm the one who's finally going to change someone, I may be the one who gets victimized.
- My life will improve when I stop waiting for a rescuer, and begin to rescue myself.
- I can learn to act in the best interests of a relationship without neglecting my own best interests.
- I can own my own power wherever I am, wherever I go, whomever I'm with.
- I will surround myself with people who are learning to live and enjoy their own lives.
- I can take responsibility for myself. I don't have to take responsibility for other people.
- I need love, but I don't need destructive love.
- Controlling keeps me from enjoying other people, and it blocks their growth.

## Self-esteem

- Being a victim is the path of least resistance.
- I can trust myself. I am wiser than I think.
- I will strive to be all that I can be.

- I'm the most important person in my universe.
- I can learn something worthwhile every day of my life.
- Life is not over till it's over.
- A strong person is not always big, but a big person is always strong.

**Peace**

- Walking on eggshells makes an irritating sound. I don't have to do it.
- Denial is when I pretend my circumstances are something other than what they are.
- I can learn to recognize when I'm reacting, rather than responding.
- When I've done all I can do, it's time to let go.
- When I'm feeling in chaos, I need to say and do as little as possible so I can restore my peace.
- I can ask for what I want and need. If I don't get it, I can figure out what to do next.
- Let go and let God.
- One day at a time.
- During stressful times, I can rely more heavily on my support system.
- Just for today, I will be strong enough to accept anything that comes my way.
- Today is the first day of the rest of my life.
- I will learn to use my head before I use my words.

***

Photocopy these suggestions or write each one on a piece of paper and tape them to your bathroom mirror. Hopefully you have a mirror large enough to hold all the wonderful new messages you will be taping over the next few months. Look through magazines, newspaper articles and one day at a time calendars. Listen to other people's wisdom and if something strikes you with a ring of healthy truth, write it down and put it on your mirror.

Read your messages every morning as you face yourself in the mirror. Little by little, you will be reprogramming yourself. Something magical happens with mirrors. It is as if you are literally taking these words of truth and planting them deep inside you. Like the childhood fairy tale: *Mirror, Mirror on the Wall, Who's the Fairest of Them all*, in time you will discover, *you are.* Treat these messages as valuable jewels, for the change they will bring has the highest value of anything you will ever acquire.

In times of stress, search your mirror for that particular truth that reflects the situation you are troubled about. As time goes on, you'll find that sooner or later everything you need to get well will show up on that mirror. Your unconscious mind will begin searching throughout your day for what you need. Eventually, you'll listen to what wise people say, and there, too, you will acquire words for your mirror, especially as you move across that bridge and begin spending time with healthy people.

There is an old Chinese proverb: If you provide fish for a man, he will have food for a day; if you teach a man to fish, he will have food for life. In building your Magic Mirror, you are giving yourself food for life.

## Journalizing

Writing your most private thoughts on paper on a daily basis is an excellent way to stay in touch with your inner self as well as an opportunity to access places that will illuminate the truth. You will need a safe place to store it. Without a sense of safety and privacy, you may find yourself editing and deleting thoughts that will bring you the most help. If your partner is not to be trusted, leave your journals with someone who is, until you are ready to confront a decision about your partner. There should be nothing too sacred or too personal for you to write about. Writing enables you to see the truth more clearly. Keep remembering the screaming child inside you who is waiting for your love. Treat your journal as if it is your best friend, one that can not only keep a confidence, but knows how to maintain silence when you want to speak. A password-locked file on a computer is a good option.

## Draw Pictures with Your Non-Dominant Hand

Find a quiet time and a safe place. Gather crayons and blank sheets of paper. Whether you have talent or not, begin drawing pictures of your life, starting at the age of two, with your left hand (if you are right handed. If you are left handed draw the pictures with your right hand). Draw pictures at one-year intervals, of the first thing that comes into your mind. Use crayons to depict emotions, blue for sad times, black for grief, red for fear and anger, yellow and green for happiness. Let your mind float through the memories you draw. If you don't remember anything at that age, use your imagination from family stories you have heard to recreate a possible scene. Search through family photos and speak with relatives about events that happened when you were a child. Leave no stone unturned.

The unconscious mind stores an incredible amount of information, and what you draw based on other people's information may not be that far off. If you are utilizing the services of a competent therapist, take your pictures to your next session. The two of you can discuss their significance. If you are working without a therapist, choose a time when you are well rested, have a full stomach, and are not in the middle of a stressful problem. Sit in a quiet place where you can examine each one. Write below the picture what you think it means, and how that particular scene has impacted your adult life. If you have a safe family member who was a part of that scene, show the picture to them and get their input. It may prove invaluable.

## Talk into a Recorder

You are now ready to travel through time in an even more revealing manner. Invest in a voice-activated tape recorder, digital voice recorder, or use a headset on your computer. Talk into the recorder about your life, your childhood, your feelings, your problems and possible solutions. Talk about your hopes and wishes now, and what they were when you were little. Search through your life as if you were looking for missing pieces, for in truth, you are. Nothing is too unimportant to talk about.

Play the recordings back and listen to everything you've said. Try to be fair-minded and realistic about what was abuse and what was not. If you can remember a time before your abuse happened, talk about that. Remember the good, the healthy parts to your childhood. Did you have an uncle who treated you with love and consideration? Talk about him. Was your grandmother nurturing and supportive? Remember her. Talk about the pain of all that happened whether it was related to your abuse or not. It will prove not only cathartic but you may find explanations for how you were set up to be molested. Drag all the ghosts into the light and look at them.

If it helps, label the PM (**Pre M**olestation) time and the AM (**A**fter **M**olestation) time. What you are trying to do is reach across the trauma to the time before it happened. That is where your inner child lives, waiting for you to get healthy. Eventually, you will need to connect the two of you. Talking to yourself and listening back to all that your life was will build a picture. There you will locate all the missing parts. Your life will then be complete. The use of your hand-held recorder will begin the healing process, exposing all the demons. Listening back is the key.

## Hypnosis

For some victims who have no memory or only shadowy memories, hypnotherapy, coordinated with the efforts of your primary therapist, can be a great help. Hypnosis taps into the unconscious mind, the receptacle of all that has happened in our lives. Not everyone is a candidate for this sort of therapy for a variety of reasons, and for those who aren't, it would aid them little. This is not usually discovered until you begin to undergo the actual hypnosis. But if you are receptive, it can be a tremendous aid in recapturing memories needed to see the complete picture.

The memories can be searing, so prepare to enter unpleasant territory. It may not even be cleansing, but it will be revealing. Give thought as well as much discussion with your primary therapist before entering this realm. Weigh and balance the need for it. For some, it becomes the final argument that the abuse really happened and the one thing needed to surge ahead with the truth. For others, it brings to the fore realities they'd prefer not to have in their head. The choice is yours. Take into account the wisdom of your therapist before making that decision.

## Making a list of your shame: healthy and unhealthy

While you are in recovery, you will hear a lot about shame, that feeling of humiliation that stems from guilt. There are two different kinds of shame: healthy and unhealthy. Healthy shame, a result of our own actions, is a positive motivator. If you badmouth a friend in a moment of anger, the guilt prompts shame, which brings about a need for restitution and a restructuring of what you discuss. When you work your way through the Twelve Steps, you will learn how to deal with healthy shame without feeling less of a person. As time goes on, you will see healthy shame as a valuable tool for removing negativity. In addition, it will give you the courage to face many day-to-day situations that used to cause you embarrassment. When combined with courage and assertiveness, it brings great strides in your confidence as well as the growth of your soul.

Unhealthy shame, on the other hand, is that secret part of us that feels such low self-worth that we become immobilized. No other word so aptly describes the one attribute that keeps child sexual abuse secret. This kind of shame is the direct result of other people's actions. As is usually the case when dealing with the action of another, this one is more difficult to overcome and more painful. Instead of adjusting our behavior patterns to keep an uncomfortable event from repeating, we have to depend on an adjustment in others. Sometimes, modifying our behavior will generate that adjustment, causing the shame to pass.

Shame caused by sexual abuse does not pass that easily. Upon that original shame we build years of additional shame, locking it into that closet in our minds, until the burden becomes unbearable. Trying to live a healthy life while you are buried in shame is impossible. That shame is the infection that needs to be lanced. When someone belittles us in public or rebuffs a kindness in front of co-workers, shame crawls like a physical discomfort over our body. It tells something about them, not about us. However, untreated sexual abuse victims have such low self-worth that they are unable to see this. Once recovery is completed, your response to such actions comes from a place of strong self-esteem. You will be able to foil such opponents with "I" statements such as "I'm sorry you feel that way. Perhaps we can talk privately once you are feeling better." The more you practice this, the easier it becomes. Eventually you will almost welcome any challenge to your ability to turn a negative comment or action into a positive response. The resultant feeling of confidence empowers you. Personal power is one of the primary purposes of recovery. With that one quality you can be and do anything you want.

Make a list of your shame, all those things you've done over the years that weigh heavily on your shoulders. Once you enter a Twelve Step Program, you will be doing this in more detail. Don't just list the things you did, list what others have done to you. This exercise is to get your feet wet and begin seeing the results of what happened to you when you were younger. Mostly, it is an attempt to see the truth. Armed with this, you can begin making quantum leaps in self-confidence.

**Things I've done that caused shame.**

_____

_____

_____

_____

_____

_____

**Things others have done to me that caused me shame.**

_____

_____

_____

_____

_____

_____

The things you've done over the years that brought guilt are probably a direct result of being molested. Let this be your own examination of conscience. Don't be afraid. Confession really is good for the soul. An amazing thing happens once you face those demons. You live through it, and become stronger as a result. The more you write about your shame, the more it will diminish. Your self-esteem will grow in direct proportion to the release of your shame.

You need do nothing more than to write it down. This is a cleansing process, and later on when you go through a Twelve Step program, you'll rid yourself of all of that shame. It was never yours to begin with and you will learn to place it squarely in the lap where it belongs, your perpetrator's.

## Attend Seminars

Many groups in your area provide help for childhood traumas. Check newspapers and college bulletin boards. Look for flyers at your Twelve Step meetings that advertise seminars and groups. Check hospitals, churches, doctor's and therapist offices for other flyers. Recovery is everywhere.

You are fortunate, for never before at any time in the history of man have so many options been available for mental and emotional health. A hundred years ago, there were no Twelve Step programs, no therapists, no books available for recovery, and no John Bradshaw. Even fifty years ago, there were almost no tools to help with sexual abuse recovery, and post recovery was a term unheard of. As short a time as thirty years ago, there was still little help available for recovery. Therapists poked around in your brain with almost no answers and no desire to look at the hard subjects. There are few opportunities to improve if the topic is seldom discussed. Even today, one can find motion pictures filled with sex and violence that draw the public in droves, while movies with incest or other child sexual abuse as its central theme die a rapid death. The subject is too difficult and too shameful for most people to deal with. This program, REPAIR, is a soft focus on that hard subject.

Remember, as I said earlier, that if you find yourself in a group or at a seminar that is beginning to feel uncomfortable, do not be afraid to walk away. Trust your inner voices; they do not lie. Not all recovery groups are healthy. They mean to be, but are often misguided. Speak out when you are uncomfortable. If your questions are not answered to your satisfaction and you are still leery, leave and discuss your feelings and thoughts with your therapist or a Twelve Step group where you'll feel safe.

## Work A Rigorous Twelve Step Program

Working the Twelve Steps is vital in making your way across the bridge. For almost seventy years, they've had a proven track record to be almost miraculous in their recovery rate. But it is not sufficient to just attend meetings. Only in working the steps, one after another in the order in which they were designed, will you receive their full benefit.

Take your time. It may be as much as a year or longer before you work your way through the first. But you will find that as you proceed they get easier, not harder. Each one is designed to build strength and prepare you for the next. If you have ever heard anyone describe the "spiritual awakening" you receive at Step Twelve, you too will want to make your way to that step. It is an incredible experience that can only be felt after completing the other eleven steps.

Another way of accessing help is in finding a sponsor. This is a fellow Twelve-Stepper who has already been through the program and is willing to guide you as you do your own Twelve Step work. Utilizing the services of a sponsor is a personal choice. Some function fine with only a therapist as a guide, and others will need a sponsor. If you don't have a therapist, you will probably need a sponsor. Part of the tradition in Twelve Steps is to reach out to help others. If you feel comfortable about it, write down phone numbers from the other members and utilize the network you create for a support group that can clearly identify with what you are going through. Others, uncomfortable with this, are more loners. There again, it is a personal choice. Each of us is different and this may be another part of your own rhythm, a topic we will discuss later. Check your library and/or book stores. You will find a wealth of media and books that prove excellent guides in working your way through the steps. You are never alone in any part of this program. In addition, many Twelve Step meetings provide literature free of charge or at a minimal cost.

## Create a Family History

Creating a family history is an important part of your recovery. Through it you will see a pattern that helps to access the truth. Once you discover the dysfunctional family members in your history, you'll understand that raising a healthy child with those tools was an impossible task. A womanizing grandfather would definitely have sent wrong messages to his children. A grandmother

who was an adult-child (an adult who never went
through all the developmental stages necessary to be a
fully functioning adult) paired with a patriarchal husband would have developed co-dependent ways. If she
had alcoholic brothers that she coddled and made excuses for, the lineage who witnessed this would have an
incorrect concept of how unhealthy being an alcoholic
really is. The list goes on and on. Once you follow your
generations back through time, you'll discover that you
were a disaster waiting to happen. The power of this
knowledge is in the realization that it wasn't your fault.
You were set up.

1. List all members of your nuclear (birth) family, starting with the oldest (parents) down to the youngest. Include yourself.

_____

_____

_____

_____

_____

_____

2. List mother's parents. _____

_____

3. List father's parents. _____

_____

4. List any aunts or uncles, grandfathers or grandmothers who lived with your birth family during your growing-up years.

_____

_____

5. List any known boundary violation behavior patterns that any family members may have exhibited, i.e., fondling inappropriate parts of your body, lewd suggestions and/or inappropriate remarks, etc. (no matter how minor) and who it was.

_____

_____

_____

6. List any comments you may have heard over the years regarding any of the above family members that would indicate they had boundary violation behavior patterns. Example: in my case, the well-known comment about my paternal grandfather was, "No woman is safe with him."

_____

_____

_____

_____

7. List any known sex offenders in the family, whether criminally prosecuted or not. If none, write "not applicable."

_____

_____

_____

8. Draw (using stick figures if necessary) the history of your family. Mark the members with inappropriate boundary violations with a red color. Mark yourself with a blue one. Draw a circle around the ones that could have protected you but didn't for whatever reason. Draw yourself in the middle and the others in varying degrees of closeness to you.

***

Creating a family history may entail traveling to relatives to ask questions. Some will be cooperative, others not. Explain honestly what you are going through and the help you need. Pay close attention to any revelations concerning unhealthy behavior of your parents, grandparents and great-grandparents. Go as far back as you need. If letters are available, study them. You'd be surprised what the written words of others reveal about their inner selves. Often we will put on paper what we don't have the courage to speak out loud. Act as if you were a reporter gathering information for a story. In a way you are—yours.

**Write a letter** (to your perpetrator and your parents—if you feel they betrayed you by not protecting you.)

Don't be afraid to write down everything that is inside of you. A picture is emerging by now—from reading books, journaling, listening to CDs or tapes, doing some of the exercises and talking into your voice recorder. You will have a lot to share. In doing this, you will be taking the shame off your shoulders and laying it squarely where it belongs. This exercise will cause a lightening of the heart. Once you give something away, it is no longer yours.

If parents/perpetrators are deceased, travel to their graves. Sit on the earth and have a heart to heart talk about the pain and the shame that was handed to you so many years ago. Get angry. Speak out loud about what their actions cost you. Leave nothing untouched. This will prove to be the catharsis that allows you to forgive and let go of the past.

## Tips To Help You In The Midst Of Your Journey

**Remember HALT: Hungry Angry Lonely Tired.** Whenever you are having difficulty coping, remember to check this list. If any one of these is present, taking care of those needs will bring immediate emotional relief.

**The Attitude of Gratitude**—Daily list all your blessings in your mind. Everyone has some even though they may seem unimportant. Do you like to read? How about the movies? How about a special friend? Do you have lovely hands? A high energy level? Are you warm and affectionate? Do you like your job? If not, do you like your co-workers? Dig, dig, dig. You will find many more than you realized. Write them down. Something magical happens. Your blessings will begin to increase. And as they increase, so will your optimism about life and all its promises. These blessings will be an oasis in the midst of your journey across that bridge.

**Create your own repertoire of "courage songs."** Throughout the ages, people have adopted songs that gave them courage to keep living no matter how dark the times looked. Songs like *Ol' Man River, Deep River, Battle Hymn of the Republic, Swing Low Sweet Chariot, When you Walk Through A Storm, Amazing Grace,* and even our national anthem are courage songs. The songs are stirring, give us hope, and bind us to a promise. Find some of your own and whether you sing or not, use the words to give you courage. You will be surprised how much stronger you'll feel.

**Listen to John Bradshaw's recordings**—over and over.

**Pamper yourself**—by indulging in something that makes you feel good: an evening walk, lunch with a friend, buy flowers for no reason, schedule a massage therapy or spa visit, curl up with a good book, write a letter to someone you love telling them how well you are doing and all the new things you're learning.

**Write a letter to your inner child**—that small you who is waiting for the two of you to meet.

**Take your life one day at a time,** one hour at a time, and, if necessary, one minute at a time.

**Call a supportive friend** and share everything you're feeling.

**Make a "wish list" of all you want to do with the rest of your life.** Don't worry about whether it's realistic or not, just write it down. When you begin asking the universe for your dreams, it starts paying attention, for the world loves persistence and rewards those who practice it.

## Learning To Deal With the Trust Issue

One of the most anguishing results of being sexually violated at a young age is the betrayal of trust. An unspoken understanding in the universe is that when one gives birth to a child, one is responsible for their wellbeing and must take that challenge seriously. Unfortunately, not everyone does. When a child is born, they look to their parents for protection against any unpleasantness. When the parent is either the perpetrator of unpleasantness or the unwilling partner to its happening by virtue of doing nothing, it is a betrayal. One of the byproducts is a child who grows up unable to trust anyone. Why should they? The world has become a scary place where we wish everyone wore a black or a white hat, depending on what role they are playing. Unfortunately they don't.

How does one cope with the inability to trust? Learning to differentiate between the bad guys and the good guys is a step in this direction. Setting boundaries buys you time to gain more information that enables you to do this. Learning to rely on your own inner voices is another. Learning to place the blame for that mistrust where it belongs is a third. These things will happen as you move through this program. As your own emotional and mental maturity develops, you will gain the confidence to make choices that impact, whether or not you are in a safe place. Practice will eventually enable you to remove yourself from any situation that reeks of potential harm. Taking your time in getting to know others will add to your feeling of safety. Much of this will come together when we arrive at the Awareness part of our program.

## Boundary Setting

Once you cross that bridge, you will be ready to empower yourself. You will learn a sense of restraint. It will not be easy in the beginning. Like any new behavior, practice makes perfect. As you grow in confidence and your self-esteem increases, having a sense of restraint will in time become second nature. The immediate gratification that so many wounded children go through will begin to feel like downright foolishness, especially when you count up the many times it got you in trouble. Being a victim is about giving your power and control to another. Curbing your impulses (restraint) is about giving yourself that power.

Think about ways to empower yourself with boundaries. Examples: Buy a shirt that says *What part of NO don't you understand?* Wear it often, especially around

Boundary
Setting

Unhealthy people
& Messages

those who try to control you. If you can't find one, put the words on your Magic Mirror so you will be reminded to use them when others try to wear you down with their own persistence. Practice saying "no." Simple statements such as, "Why do you ask?" or "That's kind of a personal question," are great for setting boundaries. "

"I'll get back to you" or "Let me think about it," are ways to stall people who demand instant answers and ask questions that are too personal. Give yourself time before making decisions. You have the right to take as much time as you want. No one has the right to bully or manipulate you into responding to their needs. Learn to recognize the signs of manipulative and controlling people. Passive/aggressive behavior, game playing, whining, laying guilt trips, and dragging out "old stuff" that has already been resolved are only a few of their tactics. If you do not respond, they will soon give up. Unhealthy behaviors like these require more than one person to play.

Do not give away your power. You have earned it. *Get stubborn* about your own rights. No one else's demands are anywhere near as important as your own. We're not talking about selfishness; we're talking about survival.

Boundary setting will encourage a survivor of childhood sexual abuse to deal in a healthy manner with one of the most prominent emotional difficulties they have, anger. Being angry at your perpetrator is not only normal, but healthy. At the time of your original trauma as a child, you weren't able to feel the anger, much less deal with it. As years went by, the anger has accelerated until nothing short of murder feels comfortable. It's time to deal with the anger. If for no other reason, holding onto anger can cause serious physical ailments. Unresolved conflicts—anger is one—turn inward. Once they turn inward, you are forcing your body to deal with the emotional pain and it will not have enough energy to deal with your physical health. Your immune system will weaken. Are you willing to give your perpetrator (and the anger you feel) the power to damage—perhaps permanently—your body? Who would win in the end? Certainly not you.

Letting go of your anger is vital to the healing process. As you learn boundary setting, you will feel stronger. Feeling stronger alleviates some of the anger. Knowing that you cannot go back and change what happened but that you can go forward into a healing mode helps. Once you see the overall picture, especially the family history, it will be easier to approach this step.

Make a list of ways to create boundaries.

**I will empower myself by:**

_____

_____

_____

_____

## To Feel Is To Heal

Some of us feel that we have cried enough tears to drown the world. We may have. Others have lived in a shell of stony emotions all their lives, unable to feel even the good. If you've never cried before, you will learn to do so now. Whether you cried before or not, the tears you have now will not be of anger, fear, and frustration, but tears of genuine sorrow—a healing kind of sorrow. As you move through the pain, as you see the complete picture, and especially, as you meet your inner child, all the feelings will contribute to bringing together that fragmented part of yourself that exploded at the moment of trauma.

Learn to identify your feelings. Periodically throughout your day, ask yourself *what am I feeling right now?* In time, this will arm you with reality on what is the appropriate response for each situation that occurs. Anger requires setting boundaries; fear involves finding a supportive friend to share it with, wise insights on why you're afraid and what you can do to offset it; joy promotes well-being and illustrates more clearly that life is good; and so on. Identifying feelings and their appropriate responses not only empowers and strengthens you, it has the added reward of making you feel centered and stable. The more you do this, the more it will become second nature.

## Meeting Your Inner Child

**"What lies behind us and what lies before us
are tiny matters compared to what lies within us."**

When Ralph Waldo Emerson wrote those words, the concept of the inner child was still part of the future. The power of that which lies within us, which includes our inner child is awesome. You are now ready to meet that lost child who has been waiting all these years for you to realize she exists. Start by collecting family photos of yourself at a young age, in particular of the time before you were violated. Study them. Put them next to your bed where you can see them upon awakening. Look at them frequently and as you do, try to remember what you were doing and what took place at the time the photo was taken. If you can't remember, create a memory; it may not be that far off. Sometimes talking to supportive family members about photos from the past will jog their memory and give you more information.

Choose a place where you may have spent happy time as a child: a park, a playground, a beach, an empty field, etc. If you had none, create one in your mind. Being near things of God (mother nature) will help you in this. Close your eyes and sit quietly. Travel back in your mind through the years until you arrive at that place where your inner child dwells. Think about what it must be like to once having been happy and carefree and then be locked in a prison. Picture being frightened and alone as a child inside the body of a grownup. Picture that child

wanting desperately for the grownup part of her to ac-
knowledge her existence.

Slowly, your child will step out of the shadows. This
will not happen overnight. You may spend weeks at that
park waiting for your inner child to come forth. He has
spent years in hiding and needs to learn to trust that
you are serious about bringing him into a safe place.
Why should he come out to meet you, only to find more
pain waiting?

Meeting your inner child

Once your inner child sees that you are doing every-thing in your power to turn your life around, she'll be ready. Reach out and embrace her. Tell her you love her and you are sorry to have turned your back on her all these years. Weep with her for all the sad times. Then let her know that you are working on getting well and that one day she will stop crying, she will be free and happy.

For the next few weeks spend time with that inner child in your place of happy childhood memories. Talk with her about all that had happened—all the despairing times, no matter how small. As she treads painfully through each, give her a hug and tell her that while you weren't there for her then, you are now. Bond with that inner child in your mind as much as you can. You are taking missing pieces of your life and connecting them as you would create the picture from pieces to a puzzle. As you do this exercise, you will remember things you had long forgotten. Assembling these pictures will even-tually make you a whole person, instead of fragmented. Eventually, as the months pass, you will one day realize that your inner child is now the same age as you. When this happens, it brings great inner strength and personal power.

You are now ready to enter the next step, Awareness!

| 6 | Awareness |  |
|---|-----------|---|

**Understanding, is the key,**

*Acceptance is the door.*

Socrates, one of the world's greatest philosophers, once said, "An unexamined life is not worth living." Much truth lies in those words as well as much power. In this chapter you will need to draw on this to understand the importance of *Awareness*.

The quality of becoming aware includes many components. Sensibility, prudence, knowledge, visualization, feeling, and foresight are a few. They are siblings in the same family, gifts given to humans at birth. With these gifts, a human can be and do all to which they aspire. Let's take a closer look at these qualities before we proceed to see what part they played in our childhood sexual abuse issue.

### Properties of Awareness

| | |
|---|---|
| Sensibility | Visualization |
| Prudence | Feeling |
| Knowledge | Foresight |

## Sensibility

One of the marks of sensibility is the capacity to reason, to use your head and think things through. It is an invaluable tool to have by your side as you journey through life. A sensible person makes wiser decisions. He doesn't react, he responds. He knows he can take all the time in the world to make a choice, and because he can, he makes the best choice possible.

## Prudence

Without reason or sensibility, one cannot have prudence. Prudence is cautious, not headstrong and impulsive. Prudence doesn't get one in situations that leave scars, because it's skilled in good judgment and knows all the resources available. Prudence uses that reason to discipline itself and once disciplined, life falls into order rather than chaos. One finds peace and tranquility, in that order.

## Knowledge

Knowledge gathers experiences and sorts through them for the right answers. Knowledge is cognizant of the full range of truths available in one's life. Knowledge investigates, observes and studies both human nature and the nature of things. This extends to the nature of the universe. In the gathering of this knowledge one gains power, especially personal power.

## Visualization

The ability to see all that you know, bringing it to life so that you can choose your next step, is a rare but not impossible quality. Vision, throughout the ages has progressed men from the humblest backgrounds to some of the greatest positions on earth. On a smaller scale, visualization forms mental images that propel us into our dreams. Without visualization, we have no dreams. Create a vision, then step into it.

## Feeling

The capacity to respond emotionally to everything that happens in our life is a strength, not a weakness. People who are aware of what is happening in their universe can feel. Feelings bond us to others, give us drive, protect us against wrongs, offer the gifts of humor, pathos, joy, and sorrow. Even sorrow has a healing property necessary to becoming a whole person. It is not feelings that get people in trouble, it is the actions they take based on those feelings.

## Foresight

This simple act of looking forward takes us from the past to the present and into the future. We can do nothing about what has gone before, but the present, although elusive and shifting, is the arena of change. Healthy choices made in the now will open a future that promises the fulfillment of your God-given potential.

***

Now let's take a look at these Awareness gifts inherent to man and see where they fit into the life of a person who was sexually abused as a child. They don't. When you're living in a world filled with chaos and trauma, moving from one crisis to another, the sibling qualities of Awareness can do little good.

**Sensibility**—how can a person filled with despair begin to put pieces together to find answers that make sense?

**Prudence**—once sexually molested, reacting rather than responding to the daily happenings in our lives is the only tool we know to use, thereby eliminating prudence. Good judgment is a luxury we cannot afford.

**Knowledge**—One who is sexually abused as a child may instinctively know the answers but is unable to follow through with the right choices. Knowledge only becomes a powerful tool when utilized in conjunction with the other properties of Awareness.

**Visualization**—Who can see anything but hopelessness when all you hear is a child screaming inside you, when all you know is that nothing ever works out for you?

**Feeling**—The wounded child has plenty of feelings, all of them either out of control or locked into that closet in their mind for fear that, once unleashed, they would be uncontrollable.

**Foresight**—The emotional growth of a child who has been sexually abused is locked in time at the moment of their trauma. There is no foresight for them, for they see no future, only a despairing past and a chaotic present.

This is what childhood sexual abuse has done, robbed us of these six God-given rights. It is our hope that by the time you arrive at this part of REPAIR, you will begin to experience the joy that the components of Awareness bring. They come little by little. One day you realize that you've just set a boundary to give yourself time to make a decision. Knowledge combined with prudence and accompanied by foresight gave you a useful tool. What a great step! It's time for another.

Your decisions seem wiser, partially a result of sensibility. Your old friends (those whose own lives are consumed with the same chaos and despair you used to have), may have become annoyed at you for not being "yourself," and begin to fall away. As they do so, an amazing thing happens. You don't miss them. You'll begin to realize that you're on a different road now and you have nothing in common. You'll also begin making friends who are on the same road, thereby enhancing your ability to complete REPAIR.

As you move through the program and assemble the pieces to your life, a picture emerges—the pieces to the puzzle that your life has become.

Now it's time to take a look at the other influences on a child who has been sexually abused, the family systems ones. This is the forest that your trees (the individual aspects) grew under. In order to assemble the puzzle, check which of the following family systems fit into your picture.

| Family System Checklist | |
|---|---|
| Patriarchal (or matriarchal) family system | |
| Obedient/co-dependent mother (father) | |
| Religiously regimented household | |
| Eldest daughter | |
| Alcoholic (or other addicted) parent: Mother [ ] Father [ ] | |
| Family history of sexual boundary violators | |

Write a few words about how you think any checked item impacted your life while you were growing up. Was it positive or negative? In which way?

_____

_____

_____

_____

_____

Write about how you think it changed your behavior as an adult.

_____

_____

_____

_____

_____

Now, let's take a look at each one.

## Patriarchal (Matriarchal) family

Most dysfunctional families have both a strong link and a weak one. In a home where sexual abuse occurs, the strong link is usually the father if the home is patriarchal by nature, the mother if it's matriarchal. The supremacy of the father or mother goes a long ways toward promoting obedience, the primary quality needed to be a victim of child sexual abuse. The common denominator here is someone in a position of power who has the character defect of abusing that power.

The weak link is the victim, the child who has been trained almost from birth to do what he is told without question. An obedient child is a sitting duck for a perpetrator.

In a healthy environment, a child learns discipline, not obedience. He is encouraged to say no, to speak his mind, to have his own ideas, concepts, goals, and personality. Through this, he is able to grow, not only physically, mentally, spiritually and emotionally, but in maturity as well. Even in a patriarchal family, the head of the household has responsibilities, not power. In a healthy environment he provides guidance, knowledge, wisdom, caring and discipline.

In an unhealthy environment, that weak link is exposed to situations where anything other than total obedience is punishable. The child is no match for the power of the patriarch. As the patriarch continues to be obeyed, his power grows, for whatever we feed becomes a monster. Fed by this enormous ego, the perpetrator pushes through any boundaries a child/victim could even begin to set, as well as any accepted rules of the society in which he lives.

Were you the child of a patriarchal (or matriarchal) home? Did your patriarch abuse his responsibilities? List situations other than your sexual abuse where you were powerless as a child.

_____

_____

_____

_____

_____

## Obedient/co-dependent mother (father) with weak boundaries,

[This parent may or may not have been sexually violated themselves.] All positives have a negative, all yins a yang, and so the patriarchal father (or mother) usually has an obedient partner. Frequently in the life of a child who has been sexually abused, that partner was also an untreated sexual abuse victim who had weak boundaries and was so wounded that they were unable to protect their child or fight back against the patriarch.

Every family has unspoken rules. Prior to the '60s, most families had an unspoken value system that proclaimed, "The father makes the decisions, is the ruler of all that happens in this house; the mother carries out his orders and sees to it that the value system is perpetuated." In the '40s, one of the unspoken rules regarding the patriarch was, "Even when he's wrong, he's right." They lived and died by this rule. So deeply ingrained were these rules that even seeing the reality of their own child being used for sexual purposes by their husband was not strong enough for most women to break through that obedient state and protect their child. Sometimes, turning against the child was safer.

Co-dependents have certain characteristics, some of which I mentioned earlier. The following is a checklist.

| Co-dependency Symptoms Checklist | |
|---|---|
| They place other people's needs above their own. | |
| They are afraid to set and keep boundaries. | |
| They allow their mate to control them. | |
| They are afraid to ask for what they need. | |
| They are afraid to say what they're feeling. | |
| They are the giver in the relationship. This makes them angry. | |
| They are unhappy in the relationship and feel trapped. | |
| They hate the idea of solitude. | |

| | |
|---|---|
| They feel rejected if their mate spends time away from them. | |
| Unable to control their own pain, they try to control everyone around them. | |

Did your mother or father have any traits from this list?

Write about how it felt to have a parent like this. Do *you* have any of the above traits?

## Religiously Regimented Household

One of the most frequent common denominators of child sexual abuse victims (especially in the case of incest) is that of growing up in a religiously regimented household. We are not speaking of a spiritual environment. We are talking about one that contains a strong element of hypocrisy. This false appearance creates incredible confusion in a child. A confused child is a weakened child. A weakened child is easy prey. Regimentation requires rigidity as its primary element, and when you grow up in an environment that lacks flexibility, you have no opportunity for growth. The child who cannot grow because of the unyielding and inflexible core contained in his family loses not only his freedom, but becomes locked in a world where he has no knowledge of what the truth is. Without the truth you have no life of your own; you literally become a puppet or a pawn on a chess board.

Religious training that requires rigidity also fosters control. Armed with control and a lack of flexibility, the perpetrator sets up total obedience as the only choice for the child. When you add the reality that this same child places their perpetrator on a pedestal, you now have an almost hopeless situation.

Idolizing a perpetrator at an early age is a mental attitude that follows into adulthood, especially if its origin
lies in a religiously regimented household. That perpetrator represents God. We don't know how not to idolize
him. And so we speak of him in larger-than-life terms.
"He was so handsome that women swooned; his talent as
a pianist exceeded all else; we thought he was God;" etc.
etc. are common statements made by victims about their
perpetrators once they reach adulthood. Often, they have
a lifelong need to find another they can place on a pedestal. Seeing people as they really are is difficult. If they
could realistically see members of the opposite sex, they
would not make such unhealthy choices in that area. In
order to change this behavior, it is important to first see
your perpetrator clearly. This is difficult, but not impossible.

A man's sexual needs are sometimes not met within a
marriage. As unbelievable as it may seem, this is more
likely to lead to incest than adultery for a religiously
regimented potential perpetrator. That is a sin against
the sixth commandment. But sleeping with your daughter is not. The old joke about "incest being alright as long
as you keep it in the family," despite being said in jest, is
another of the unspoken rules.

What is saddest of all is the loss of that spirituality
you might have obtained had you been raised in a family
that valued the Golden Rule and not the hell and dam-
nation code they lived by. What chance does a child in
this family have to fight back, or to develop her own innate sense of goodness?

Were you raised in such a household? Was God a
fearful God? Did He wear a face similar to your perpetrator? How did your perpetrator use religion as a whip to

crack you into obedience? What would your life have been like in a spiritual nest rather than a controlled religious environment? Write about these things. Read your own answers back. If it helps, use your voice recorder rather than your pen. The important thing is the words— these words will tap into the truth and the truth will set you free.

## Oldest Daughter

At a young age, the oldest daughter often becomes a mother figure. Being in charge of younger siblings encourages caretaking, and caretaking is one of the qualities of a co-dependent. In a healthy environment, this ability to care for others is a virtue that is tempered with maturity and strong boundaries. In a family with incest, the oldest daughter loses herself in her struggle to assume adult responsibilities she is not prepared for. All growth comes in stages. An oldest daughter who is not allowed her childhood becomes a mother symbol in the perpetrator's mind. She is now ripe for his sexual desires.

If you add to this picture the same daughter as a housekeeper, you have a person with the blueprint of an adult. As she becomes an adolescent, her budding sexuality tantalizes and tempts the perpetrator. He no longer sees her as his little girl.

## Alcoholic (Or Other Addict) Parent

While medical science is proving that genetics plays a large part in alcoholism, other factors come into play as well. The alcoholic is hiding a tremendous amount of pain, most of which no doubt stemmed from his or her own childhood trauma. More than likely, your alcoholic parent was not the first one in your family history. Statistics prove that the number of alcoholics as you go back generation after generation is enormous; in some families, almost epidemic. The very nature of alcoholism prohibits healthy behavior. In addition, the boundaries of an alcoholic are non-existent. They too may have been molested as a child, compounding their problem, and the debris that followed in its wake. If you came from an alcoholic family, the flip side was the codependent other half. You now have two common denominators in the profile of a molested person.

## A Family History of Boundary Violators

All families have skeletons in their closets. If you traveled back in time far enough, you would no doubt see at least one in every generation. This is the flawed side to human nature. No incest perpetrator arrived at his place without help. When you have children who raise children, you have an adult child. When you have a womanizer who raises a child, you create the potential for another womanizer—and so on. We are what we have been trained to become not only with the blatant, spoken messages but with subliminal ones as well. The subliminal ones are often more insidious. One person with unhealthy behavior can raise generations of unhealthy descendants.

It only takes one person to break that cycle. Man has an enormous potential for goodness. But like a tree that is not pruned, watered and fertilized, and is kept from the sun, a child without the right guidance will become wounded and pass the results of his wound to his children, his grandchildren, and their children.

The chance of boundary violators lurking in your history is great. Seek them out. Write about them. Drag them out of the holes in which they hide and expose them. Label them for what they are. If your grandfather, so idolized by his children, was a womanizer, call him so. If your father, placed on a pedestal by those who knew him, sexually violated you, he needs to be toppled. Only in the seeking and finding of the truth will you be able to make an honest appraisal of your total picture.

***

Now you are ready to begin assembling the pieces. This will rapidly bring you to the stage we are currently working on—Awareness. Find a safe place and some quiet time to meditate on all you have learned. Take a hard look, especially at the family history you have discovered. Think about the unhealthy messages and all the times in your life where you didn't have a choice. Would you have chosen differently if you could? Ask yourself searing questions and give yourself strong and sensible answers. How responsible are you for the actions of others? Tell yourself over and over: *This is a statement about them, not about me.*

Picture a chess board with all its pieces. The pawn (you as a child) is moved and motivated strictly for the self-serving interests of the king and queen (your parents and/or your perpetrator). Significant aspects to the profile of an incest family may include many things. They are all red flags. How many red flags did you have on the *Profile Of A Child Sexual Abuse Victim* that you filled out earlier? How many did you want and would you have chosen at birth? How many showed up on your *Family Systems* profile?

Now, approach this puzzle from another perspective. What if no sexual abuse had happened during your childhood, and your years had been all that you had wanted when you were younger? What would that picture have looked like? Would you have chosen as your life's partner someone supportive and caring? Would you have gone to college and become a doctor? An actress? A famous writer? Would you have traveled, had more friends, happier memories? Would your health be better? How much has the world lost in producing so many wounded children? That tiny child who was molested at the age of eight and lived a life of despair may have become a famous scientist who discovered a cure for cancer. That lovely daughter who was raped at the age of twelve may have become a renowned ballerina. Whether the molestation happened at the age of one or the age of seventeen, the trauma, unless interrupted by a strong recovery program, creates an indelible blueprint that follows their entire life.

Make a list of all that your life would have been if the trauma of sexual abuse had never impacted it. Where would you be today if this had turned out to be true? Probably not reading this book. It is not too late to have anything on your list. Remember that growing older can often be less a hindrance and more a help to your dreams. If you became wiser, more mature, more disciplined and focused, couldn't you now go to college if that had been one of the things on your list? Once you complete this program, you'll become that person. If you now could tell the bad guys from the good ones, wouldn't you make a healthier choice in a mate? It's not too late. It's only too late when you say it is.

Richard Nixon once said, "A man is not finished when he's defeated, he's finished when he quits.. Do you want to quit? Do you really want to be in the final years of your life and know that you had the opportunity to turn your life around and you failed to grasp it?

It's a proven fact that *Child molesters pick the most obedient child in the school yard.* As you progress further into recovery, you'll begin to understand this. You see yourself as that pawn in a game of chess, realizing you could not have changed your family history or the part you played in it.

List traits and behavior patterns you had prior to being molested, then list those you had as a result of being molested.

| Traits before being molested | Traits after being molested |
|---|---|
|  |  |
|  |  |
|  |  |
|  |  |
|  |  |
|  |  |
|  |  |

You are now ready for the next stage in REPAIR—the stage called Insight.

| 7 | Insight |  |

Freedom—A state man has struggled to attain
throughout the centuries—

*Is hindered only by the locks and prisons in our own mind.*

At you move through the stages of REPAIR, what was
lost in your life becomes clearer with every day that
passes, as well as the desire to regain it. The Twelve
Steps start to make sense, old messages are difficult to
access, new ones spring out automatically. Your memory
opens with things formerly hidden or lost. In the stage of
Awareness, you assembled pieces to the puzzle that your
life had become. It is time to put the pieces together so
you can see the complete picture and comprehend what
previously was obscure.

What you have been doing up to now, whether you
realize it or not, is healing. Your fragile ego has been in a
weakened condition, and then it has been battered. With
little faith in ourselves, we often do our own battering. As
you proceed through the process of REPAIR, you slowly
strengthen your self-esteem. Now you realize you are not
to blame. Over the years, your perpetrator, like Pontius
Pilate washing his hands, placed the blame for *his*
wrongdoing on you. This could have been done either directly or indirectly.

One of the ways in which he accomplished this purpose was through the use of subliminal messages.
Subliminal messages have diabolical power and take root
even more than blatant ones. If your perpetrator was
your father, his subliminal message could have been, *It's
okay to have sex with married men.* This may have been

one of the directions you followed as an adult, thereby breeding self-loathing. It is difficult to have healthy self-esteem when you feel you are covered with garbage. Another message may have been, *It's not okay to set sexual boundaries.* What subliminal messages planted themselves in your unconscious, paving the way for unhealthy behavior?

| Subliminal Messages | Behaviors I Adopted As A Result |
|---|---|
|  |  |
|  |  |
|  |  |
|  |  |
|  |  |
|  |  |
|  |  |

You were literally programmed to acquire a foreign and damaging belief system at an early age. The truth has a way of making sense, and as you move through this program, truth becomes insightful.

Your history won't contain all the causative factors and consequences of sexual abuse. You may even have others not previously mentioned in this book. You may have a different gender preference or the inability to appreciate physical contact—sometimes even to the point of aversion.

Don't worry if your traits were fewer in number than others. You have enough of them to be moving through this program for the right reasons. Not everyone is the same, nor are our reactions to things that happen in our lives. One person can have suffered the most severe abuse imaginable and struggled through it to live a healthy life. Still others may have had what they consider minimal abuse and are crippled from it. The core meaning here is the impact your particular trauma had on YOU.

A variety of reasons can contribute to the intensity that you felt in being abused. Human nature is a complex structure of many things. Some of us are more sensitive than others. Some of us are cursed (or blessed as the case may be) with vivid recall. Still others have the ability to automatically detach from whatever is happening and skim over the top of the pain of their trauma. Analytical people are not as rooted in their pain as those with a creative and/or sensitive nature.

Are these people blessed? For some it is a blessing. Others, may have missed the intensity of the pain, but they have also missed the intensity of the joy of the good things that happened. And despite the pain of childhood sexual abuse, we all have had joyful moments. Keep in mind that each of us is unique; our differences are what makes the world such an exciting place to be in. Work within your own parameters and don't attempt to walk another's path or judge another's journey.

The insight acquired by working this program will prompt you to establish a whole new belief system—your own. Along with that, you'll seek out mature behavior patterns. Test your own ability to recognize new-found maturity. Some examples are: I will not judge until I have all the evidence; When I am wrong, I will apologize; My behavior will be gracious even toward those I dislike; I will remember that life is too short to be little, etc. List some of your own and those you would like to adopt.

## Mature Behavior Patterns

|  |
|  |
|  |
|  |
|  |
|  |
|  |

The next time opportunity presents itself, practice by using one of your own mature behavior patterns. Then step back and see whether it improved the situation or not. In most cases, you will be pleasantly surprised. Find someone as a mentor whose maturity you admire. Watch their responses to life's problems and how they arrived at them. Explain that you would like their help in learning what they know. Keep in mind that perhaps they too once had a mentor and are happy to give their knowledge to others. This is one of the reasons why our world, especially in the area of mental health, is a better place to be in than it was a hundred years ago.

An important part of the essential nature of insight is our intuition, that part of us that knows and sees all truth. As you approach the end of your bridge, it will come to the foreground of your awareness level. This quality is called "listening to your inner voices." We all have them and the more we listen, the more they speak. They are all-wise and all-knowing. There is no answer you need to know that is not contained in your inner voices. As we pass through life, everything that occurs feeds into our unconscious. It may lie in wait for many years before it is utilized, but when called upon to give a command performance, the truth presents itself. But how can we hear the truth when our life is consumed with distractions, especially unhealthy ones?

From birth we are all trained to have distractions in our life. Some are necessary, but some are just ways to avoid tapping into one of our greatest resources—the inner voice—that intuition. How many obsessive talkers do you know —talk, talk, talk? That way they don't have to connect with their inner child. How about obsessive television watchers—noise, noise, noise. It is an easy way to both drown out the inner voices, and distract ourselves from what we need to turn our lives around. People who were molested have an even larger propensity for creating distractions in their lives. The greater the pain of our trauma, the greater our need for distractions to keep from feeling and seeing not only the intensity of the pain, but the consequences it brings.

We all need those occasional distractions that put balance in our lives. A continual diet of examining our own behavior would become burdensome. We need social interactions, fun activities, and goal-oriented projects in all areas to give us a balanced life. Growth in the area of the six dimensions—mental, emotional, physical, spiritual, social and financial—is necessary for a stable and fulfilling life.

Little by little, as we work through REPAIR, we begin automatically to move away from the distractions and face the pain. As we do so, we also find healthy ways to combat the discomfort. Going to a therapy session that was particularly searing is followed by a movie we'd been looking forward to. It placed balance in the midst of an emotionally fragile time. Previously, we had no tools to apply ointment to the opening of these wounds. As we adopt these new and healthier behavior patterns, a surprising thing happens: We start feeling good about ourselves. We begin feeling stronger. How did it happen? We have been moving not only across that bridge, but out of the dark and into the light. The ugly things waiting behind us seem further and further away. Dragons and demons lying in wait in the swirling waters under the bridge no longer frighten us. Of course, they don't, for we have become stronger. We did so by recognizing that the sexual abuse was not about us. It was about our perpetrator.

Somewhere during this realization of the truth, we hit a wall. Mom and Dad were not perfect. What a ghastly shock. We placed our lives in their hands and trusted that they would guide us appropriately. Not only did they not, but sometimes we have to face the reality that they didn't love us. They may have controlled us, used us, been prideful of our accomplishments in public (but abusive about them in private), fed us, clothed us, and given us a home. They may even have told us they loved us and that everything they were doing was for our own good. None of this means they loved us.

How do you treat a person you love? Real love is not punitive, it is accepting; real love does not control, it guides; real love applauds in a sincere manner; real love is there when we are troubled or in pain; real love sets examples that are healthy; real love has boundaries and encourages us to have the same.

Make a list of those qualities that you think are the "real love" attributes you would like to have received from your parents. Examples might be: They not only listen to what we have to say, but they hear us; they encourage us to be all that we can be; they tell us verbally and physically (with appropriate affection) that they care and are happy we are in their life. What qualities did you not get from your parents that are "real love" qualities?

| "Real Love" Qualities | Did I Receive or Not? |
|---|---|
|  |  |
|  |  |
|  |  |
|  |  |
|  |  |
|  |  |
|  |  |

What you are doing is recreating yourself in the way you would like to have been. You are improving in areas where you felt deficient; and validating the areas that were already healthy. Our parents may not have given us all the knowledge we needed, but they did the best they could. If your perpetrator was your parent, that is another thing. For them we make no excuses.

Keep in mind that no one is perfect. Your non-abusive parent may have had pressures you weren't aware of. If they themselves were sexually abused or had early childhood trauma of another nature and had no opportunity or awareness to work this out, they were incapable of being healthy role models. Cut them some slack as you are hoping to cut yourself slack in the realities you are facing about your own shame.

This is not to say that we are not placing the blame squarely on the perpetrator. As you worked your way through the chapter on process, you learned to get angry at your perpetrator and make him accountable for everything. We are arriving at an understanding of what really happened, the part everyone played in setting up our future, and the truth of what our life became. Here again, we see so clearly how accountable the perpetrator should have been.

The other side we also see is the clarity of our own unique qualities. Like the sun that comes out from behind the shadows after a storm, we arrive at the truth.

In the realization of this truth, we discover we have never validated these qualities. Make a list. Leave nothing out. Realize that some of these are not new, but have been a part of us for most of our lives. As an example: perhaps when you were a child you were caring and sensitive to the needs of others. That may be why your particular sexual abuse was more painful to you than to a less sensitive person. Now you can view that quality as a great gift that you have to give others.

| My Wonderful Qualities | How Long Have I Had Them? |
|---|---|
|  |  |
|  |  |
|  |  |
|  |  |
|  |  |
|  |  |
|  |  |

Take a look at your list. Remind yourself that this is a part to the complete picture that you never saw. You realize you have value. You are a whole person. You have choices. Saying no is easier. Courage develops. With it comes a healthier ego, stronger self-esteem, and wise decisions. You are approaching the end of the bridge. Can you feel the lightening of your heart?

New and exciting things begin to happen. You find, to your surprise, that you enjoy being alone. Prior to getting on that bridge, solitude was a painful choice. Of course it was. Codependency requires other people. Not only that, being alone may have meant you'd have to look at truths you'd been running from during your whole life. Now that we have validated our own worth, being alone might mean spending time with that one person whose company we enjoy more than anyone—our own. What a marvelous feeling.

Another reward we receive as we approach the end of that bridge happens gradually. When this new world begins to open for you, it will contain experiences you never noticed before. The smallest things in life bring joy. It is a joy you were unable to access previously. How can a world filled with chaos and pain present opportunities for abundance? Worse yet, it did. We didn't see them, we didn't care; we had no ability to experience or appreciate any of them. More will be said about this later on in the book, when you will literally learn to "smell the roses."

But first, let's do a very important job. Let's get rid of all our shame. Find a place of peace and strength: a mountain top, a bluff overlooking a river, a meadow, the shore of an ocean. Picture all of your shame, all the negativity you carried for so long. Symbolically place it in a large gunny sack and throw it away. Heave it into the

Throwing baggage away

universe once and for all. It was never yours to begin with. All you have done is to carry it for others who should have been carrying it themselves.

Another way of doing this is to make your list of shame. Start a fire in your fireplace, put on some soft music and burn the list, telling yourself it is no longer a part of you. You are not the sum total of what you have done. You are the sum total of who you are, and by now you recognize that who you are is very special. How do you treat a person who is special? The answer should be clear.

## Forgiveness

How does one learn to forgive the unforgivable? Better yet, why should we? It is the greatest challenge you will face as you approach the end of your bridge. It is easier to begin forgiving once you understand the concept of negative energy. When you see that anger turned inward causes physical harm to your body, you will be anxious to feel that healing property called forgiveness. Holding on to an old pain only hurts you, not the other person.

By now, seeing your family history may have given you insights into why your perpetrator turned out the way he did. Understanding is always the key to forgiveness. Not forgiving will hold on to that anger and keep you from healing fully. If you can at least arrive at understanding, it will help. Remember that forgiving does not in any way mean condoning what your perpetrator has done.

If your perpetrator is deceased, it may be easier to do this. For those whose perpetrators are still alive, you may find yourself making the decision that you can no longer be around them. That, too, is a healthy choice and yours to make. Don't let anyone tell you that you have to be in their presence. We all have the right to see who we want to, to interact with those we choose. Recognizing who is healthy and who is not is one of the things you've learned by now. That gives you the right to put it into practice.

If your perpetrator was a parent, remember that there are always friends willing to be substitute mothers and substitute fathers. Find one. You didn't choose your biological parent, but you can choose one now that you willingly give your affection to. You'd be surprised how many people would welcome the opportunity to be an "adopted" parent.

## Appropriate and Inappropriate Affection

One of the most painfully confusing things for a sexually molested person is  distinguishing appropriate from
inappropriate affection. We have little wisdom in that
area. The pain of our own experience causes red flags to
crop up at the sight of any affection between a father and
daughter (or mother and son, depending on your own issue). Even if your perpetrator was not a direct family
member but another older person in a position of power,
you may have moments of discomfort in witnessing certain physical interactions between a child and older
person. This pain can be incredibly intense, not only because fear sets in (especially if it's your own child), but
because it flashes pictures from your past you don't
want to see. This response is normal.

In trauma, those pictures that lurk in our unconscious, waiting to leap out in present-day events that
trigger them, take on more intensity than they deserve.
What seems like the pain of current events is often the
pain of old stuff. Our emotions run amok, making it difficult to see this. If our intellect tells us we are
overreacting (a common behavior pattern of childhood
sexual abuse victims), then we feel guilt at shaming what
may be an innocent interaction.

Physical affection is a marvelous thing to both watch
and experience. Even animals have theirs. But in the life
of a sexually molested person, this normal, deeply satis-
fying part of life becomes a minefield. Previous to going
through REPAIR, this may have been an issue you were
unable to deal with. Hopefully, by the time you arrive at
this part, it will be easier. By now, your "trust" issue may
be more comfortable to deal with. If this has been a
problem in your immediate family, by this part in your

program you should have learned clearer communication skills, giving you the ability to discuss your fears with your mate.

Certain guidelines should be kept in mind. Here again, common sense prevails. Tiny infants require different physical affection than a six-year-old, and a six-year-old is comfortable with different affection than an adolescent. While it may be appropriate to hold that six year old on your lap, how appropriate is it for a fifteen-year-old?

One of the first questions, and the most important, is whether or not the recipient is comfortable with the affection being given. If a twelve-year-old pulls away, cringes, or avoids affection from a parent they used to feel comfortable with, this is not necessarily a sign they've been molested. It may mean they are going through the transitional stage between child and adult and no longer want to be physical. It is important to observe the responses. Clear communication is vital. If a parent asks a child what they are and are not comfortable with, they will discover where the boundaries lie. Encourage your children to set their own boundaries and applaud their efforts.

Once a child is out of diapers and potty trained, no parent should ever have a reason to poke around in their child's private body parts. As that child grows, he becomes even more aware of what is private and what is not. A parent checking their child's temperature when they are sick is different from a parent who insists on checking out the size of their teenager's breast development.

Another important thing to remember is that our body has parts and those parts have names. When we are afraid to call our body parts by their correct names, we are implying that there is something shameful about those parts. It is not only appropriate, but necessary, to refer to the various private parts by the name they have acquired. A penis is a penis and a vagina is a vagina. To call them anything else telegraphs to our children that we must not discuss these parts. If you are concerned about your child's well-being, open communication is vital. Let your children know that these private parts belong to them and that it is okay to call them by their real name. No shame should ever be attached to the physical body that God gave us. The shame we experienced through childhood sexual abuse was not about our body parts, but about a perpetrator who violated them.

In summing up, it is important for all parties to:

- Maintain respect for the wishes of the child.
- Communicate clearly about comfort levels and anxieties.
- Use prudence in judging the actions of another,
- Learn to differentiate the present and what happened to you as a child.
- Call body parts by their correct name.

With these guidelines and the work you have done thus far in REPAIR, this issue should be less significant. Keep in mind that some things never go away. We all have moments when Father's Day may be a tough one to go through (if your father was your perpetrator). It may resurrect anger and grief, but you will learn to accept that and move through it. You may still have times when seeing a father wrap his arms around a daughter waves that red flag. But now, you can put that action in the right perspective and deal with it. While these new behavior patterns and responses don't happen overnight, they do happen.

John Bradshaw talks about the one-legged ice skater he saw in Toronto. Will you ever regain your leg? No. Will you learn how to skate? Yes. Keeping this in mind will give you balance.

You have discovered that you must crawl before walking, walk before running. *Running sets you free.* Now you are ready to arrive at the concept of Rhythm. It is one of the most exciting concepts you will ever discover and opens a world you never thought to access. You are ready to step off the bridge onto the shore beyond.

| **8** | # Rhythm |  |

**The ending of recovery
Is the beginning of the rest of your life...**

*The way it was meant to be.*

The path we took in life and the decisions we made at the crossroads were shaped by our experiences. For a sexually abused child, those experiences were a horror most people cannot imagine. Nor would they want to. People who were free to become all they wanted to be cannot know what it is like to live in a prison. In completing this program, you are releasing yourself from that prison.

Once you are free, you begin to return to one of the greatest joys all living creatures have—their own rhythm. Even animals have their own rhythm and would fight mightily against anyone who tried to take it away. If you go back far enough, you can remember waking at the same time every morning and getting tired at the same time every night. You had a time for hunger, a time for energy, and a time for languor. Being a part of that natural rhythm brought joy as well as serenity. Life, predictable and comfortable, contained meaning and purpose. It was like a dance, one where we moved freely through our own universe, bending and swaying our bodies in time to our inner voices.

Newborn children have their own rhythm. They sleep through feedings or are constantly hungry, they eat at six hour intervals instead of four, they cry a lot or they're quiet. They respond to Uncle Jake who has a delightful sense of play, or they cry when Grandma Benton comes into the room with her loud, shrill voice. Each already has a unique personality with no one in the world quite like this little person. Their rhythm is not right or wrong, only different, but it is theirs. Your rhythm may be the only thing that is truly yours.

As a child of trauma, your natural rhythm was interrupted. Sexual violation shattered the serenity of your early rhythm. A child violated at the age of one has already established a natural rhythm. Once molested, the older the child grows, the more unnatural adaptations are made to their own rhythm. They hide their intense emotions out of fear of punishment and a parent's rage. When laughing at the dinner table sends them to their bedroom without food, they learn to contain their sense of humor and playfulness. Building tunnels in the living room out of blankets and chairs, a marvelous example of a child's creative nature, causes Mom to go into a fit of anger over the mess. The child learns to stifle any other expression of creativity.

As the years go by, out of a sense of fear, rejection, and feeling "less than," the real person hides deeper and deeper until once into adulthood, little remains of that spontaneous, childlike human. The mask they wear contains a great deal of anger. Who wants to be somber when your nature flows with joy? Why pretend we are submissive when being strong-minded is the real us? Holding our bodies stiff when we inwardly crave hugs is a sad, almost anguishing part of so many humans.

Natural rhythm is just that—natural. It is the essence of who and what we are. Being able to return to it is freeing as well as strengthening. As was clearly illustrated earlier, we had gifts of awareness that could have enabled us to be and have whatever we wanted. All the tools for a happy life were taken away by the childhood sexual abuse. At birth we all had potential for the inner strength needed to deal with life's problems. As a sexually molested child, we lost it.

Let's talk about inner strength for a moment. Have you ever envied someone who appears "strong as a rock?" Have you ever wished that someone was you? With the proper application of this program, it can be. Inner strength is like a shield we wear to protect us from life's trials. There is no way you can avoid these trials, but you can program yourself to make choices that will minimize them and think of solutions that will deal effectively with them. After REPAIR, you'll be able to handle any grief that might come into your life by moving through the healthy stages from denial to anger to guilt to depression and finally to acceptance.

Strong people have the ability to make not only wise choices about the direction of their life, but have the courage to take those steps. Strong people are not afraid of the truth and can apologize when wrong without feeling shame. Remember, a strong person is not always big, but a big person is always strong. Strong people can survive the day to day problems as well as the traumatizing ones that come out of nowhere.

We're not talking about stubbornness. There's a big difference. Stubborn people are inflexible, strong people are not. Stability is a quality that all wounded children crave. Ridding ourselves of that shaking in the heart and that confusion in the mind that is a result of childhood trauma seems like an unattainable goal to one who has been molested. As you moved through this program, you began to grow. With growth comes a steadying of your own course as well as a strengthening of your inner self.

If you worked a rigorous Twelve Step Program, you learned about flexibility and honesty. You also learned about change.

Life is about change. Changing those things that are inappropriate is part of gaining confidence. Refusing to change them will almost guarantee the continuing of low self-esteem. On the other hand, keeping those qualities that are uniquely yours, the appropriate ones, is part of your natural rhythm. You don't want anything more taken away from you. You have lost enough already.

Guidelines to acquiring wisdom—thereby strength— are simple. The golden rule—*Do unto others as you would have them do unto you*—still works best. Even spiritual beliefs, as opposed to rigid religious guidelines, should be founded on this. As you approach the end of your bridge, you will make the marvelous discovery that most of the old adages are true. *A Stitch in time saves nine; Watch the pennies and the dollars will take care of themselves* will resurrect to give you wisdom. Take a hard look at all those you're aware of. Utilize what you have learned thus far to keep the good ones and discard the foolish. *Children should be seen and not heard* is an incredibly stupid statement. Our mothers would have done better to have said, *The spontaneous but disciplined child is a happy child.*

One has only to watch nature to see the importance of following your own rhythm. As the seasons change, so does that rhythm. If you follow the path of nature, you can see that rhythm is inherent in all things of God. A plant grows from a seed into a sapling, into a trunk with branches, and then bears blossoms and fruit. It has a time to shrivel and die and yet another time to be reborn. Everything in the land has a rhythm. And so it is with humans. Take a walk in a forest and observe Mother Nature. There are more truths and wisdom hidden in her depths than anyplace in the world.

As you emerge on the other side of the Bridge of Recovery, you will begin to crave your own blueprint (rhythm), the one you originally had. You will want order instead of chaos. You will think ahead rather than act on impulse. You will work through challenges knowing that when something distressing happens, *the only thing that's the end of the world is the end of the world.*

Toxic people and toxic excitement will now feel like instability and insanity. Even more gratifying is your ability to recognize these things. The discomfort acquired from being in the presence of toxicity will prompt you to arrange your life in a rhythm that brings both serenity and predictability. Predictability is not synonymous with boredom. A need for excitement through partying, arguing, drugs, alcohol, and multiple sex partners will now seem immature and dangerous in your newly established world of peace. The natural high you have heard people speak of will become a part of your life.

Everyone's rhythm is unique. Are you a morning person or an evening person? Are you hungry when you first awaken or is your appetite not stimulated until you've been up and about for hours? Do you like quiet or do you like noise? Are material possessions a need or are you Spartan? Do you fancy travel or do you like to be rooted? Are you a talker or a listener? Is your humor quiet or are you raucous and rowdy?

None of these are right or wrong, just different. We cannot all be the same and if you try to bend a branch so that it will grow in a direction contrary to its nature, it will wither and die. So it is that we must all be true to our own inner self and become a part of our innate natural rhythm.

A sense of freedom develops once you become true to your own nature. Shakespeare proclaimed: *To thine own self be true.* His words ring with truth. An environment where we are forced to do what is opposite from our natural rhythm breeds resentment. Stemming from what we perceive as a wrong or injury, it digs its own hole. Most of the time such an emotion begins with a lack of honesty.

If we tell a friend we don't mind babysitting their children, when in fact we were looking forward to attending a play, resentment settles in. You are not helping your friend or yourself by this lack of honesty. Maybe taking care of children is not your area of expertise. Perhaps suggesting another friend to baby-sit while you offer to take your friend to a play is more in line with your own rhythm. Why pretend to be what you are not? Assertiveness and honesty are needed to combat resentment.

This does not mean that it is okay to do whatever we feel like regardless of consequences; it means tempering your real nature with common sense. Laugher is vital, but is it appropriate during a church sermon or at the expense of someone else's emotional well-being? A healthy sense of discipline is important as well as a sense of fair play. Indulging oneself in strong opinions and being single-minded of purpose is admirable. How admirable does it become when we hurt others as a result of it? Have you ever heard the parents of an only child who is tearing your house apart make the comment, *"Isn't he cute? He's a natural born leader."* What's missing in this picture?

Children who have been sexually abused, as well as all wounded children, begin wearing masks at an early age. Afraid to be who they really are, they choose different masks for different encounters. That way, no one has to see their true selves. Filled with shame from childhood trauma, they don't see themselves as jewels, and slipping on the mask enables them to hide from their real selves while escaping another's disappointment or wrath. Your self-esteem will build after you go through recovery and begin locating those treasures that were always there. This gives you the courage to throw away the masks. Once the real you steps out, being unrestrained presents rapture you could scarcely imagine prior to recovery.

A good example of those who followed their own rhythm was the forefathers of America. They knew what they were doing when they journeyed across the waters to a new land. Deprived of the right to worship in the manner of their own choice, they set out to find a place where they could be themselves. In turning their backs on tyranny, they were setting boundaries as well as following dreams and goals. They knew they had choices, and coming to a land where they could explore them was the first step to individuality. Fortunately, they had the wisdom to understand that not everyone's choice was the same. Thus the United States became a land of multiple religions as well as one of tolerance and acceptance.

It is necessary to feel accepted. As a child of trauma, we only experienced acceptance when we were obedient to our parents and the world outside. While at times obedience was a necessary ingredient in making our way into adulthood, often it required limiting our choices and wearing masks that covered up the real person—literally the inner child.

Once you complete recovery, your own rhythm will begin to form. Natural behavior patterns will emerge. As layer upon layer of your true self comes together, in time you will realize that this is what you have craved since the trauma.

Picture waking up in a world where all of the choices are your own. Remember the cartoon of the woman in the three-sided cage. You have stepped out of yours into a world of freedom. If formerly you were with a mate who controlled your every move, you either will no longer be with him or he will also have begun recovery. It is impossible, once you cross that bridge, to remain in an unhealthy environment. Now your entire day will pulsate with your own rhythm. Now you can turn all the mountains into rocks, the rocks into pebbles.

Mountains turning into Rocks, rocks into pebbles

Do the following exercise to return to what you really are. Describe your natural rhythm in the following areas:

(i.e., I sleep deep or light, I snore, I hug pillows, I'm a fast talker, rowdy humor etc.)

Sleeping _____

_____

_____

Conversation _____

_____

_____

Humor _____

_____

_____

Hobbies and interests _____

_____

_____

_____

My favorite people would look like:_____

_____

_____

My favorite foods are: _____

_____

_____

_____

My value system includes: _____

_____

_____

_____

My political affiliation and beliefs are: _____

_____

_____

_____

My religious and spiritual beliefs and needs are: _____

_____

_____

_____

List other areas of your life, your likes and dislikes. Show a clear picture of everything you are the most comfortable with. How many are in your life now? Why are the others not?

Do not be uncomfortable with the fact that your rhythm is different from your mates, your siblings, your friends, or your parents. The world would be a boring place if we were all the same. Not only that, there would be no progress. It is only in our individuality that we begin discovery, and discovery is one of the most vital parts of a world that moves in harmony.

The more we choose to follow the path of our own nature, the happier we'll be. As always, this guideline must be tempered with wisdom. The ability to use common sense as a tool to navigate through life is invaluable. Unfortunately, the only thing wrong is that it isn't very common, one of the reasons the world is in such a tangle. Some of the basic rules are:

1. Do whatever works.
2. If it's not broken, don't fix it.
3. Let sleeping dogs lie.
4. Respond, don't react.
5. Choose your battles wisely.
6. Use your head before using your words.

How many others can you think of? Keep in mind that using common sense as well as staying within your own rhythm brings stability and serenity.

By now you probably see the senselessness of being judgmental. Because of the pain we carried at such a young age, the ability to accept shortcomings in others (and here we're not talking about abuse) became criticism and harsh judgments instead. Unable to look at our own behavior because of fear that we may not like what we see, we looked at others. In the process of REPAIR you came to see that not only did you learn to recognize and love the real you, but in doing so no longer had a reason to judge others. Judgments carry a heavy load. You have discovered that just because they're yours doesn't make them gospel—only the gospel according to you. With Twelve Steppers, the need to be judgmental is often softened by rephrasing it as "righteous indignation." This lends a certain humor to whatever we find not okay about another person.

Judgments are also negative. Hopefully, you have been so busy improving yourself that you've had no time to judge others. That too, brings a lightening of your load. Like a sailing ship in a race, you want to throw everything overboard that is weighing you down. Only in this will you have a better chance of finding your own rhythm.

You have been discarding a belief system handed you by your parents that was not really yours. One of the rewards of recovery is fine-tuning *your* value system. Once you perceive what is true and what is not, it will be easy to incorporate these into your life. This too makes you feel a part of your natural rhythm.

Now, the world opens up for you. You see possibilities you never thought of. If previously you only reacted to events that life presents, now you can respond. In addition, you can begin to seek out your dreams. Unencumbered with the pain of your childhood trauma, moving ahead will be your primary goal. Once a person who has been sexually abused has worked their way through recovery, they find no need to dredge up things from the past. They may always be aware of what had happened, but like a wound that has been lanced, drained of its infection, and healed with only a scar left behind, you seldom are even aware of the scar. And the

few times it comes into your mind you recognize it as
such—only a scar.

Now that you have completed the stages of REPAIR,
you are ready to find out about post-recovery.

# 9 Post-Recovery

**How do you know when it's time to leave this world?**

*When you stop learning*

Post recovery, the stage that hangs around after we complete our therapy and our Twelve Step Program, is an often neglected and fragile time. By now you've learned the tools, but you haven't necessarily used all of them. When do we arrive at this stage? Sometimes step number twelve dovetails with other events in our lives. It might be the time when we finally step away from an abusive or unhealthy relationship. Or maybe the final step gives us the courage to change jobs or move away from parents who have continued to control us—if not physically, then emotionally. Perhaps now we finally feel comfortable about having a child or writing that book or going back to college. Whatever happens, it will bring monumental changes—all for the better.

When will you be ready to discontinue therapy? Only you, with the help of your therapist, will know. Hopefully, you have been listening to your inner voices and will have developed stronger self-esteem. Along with that comes the confidence and the courage to live your own life. It's an exciting time. Your own rhythm has been established and you are in the process of finding even more of your own unique behavior patterns. It's amazing how much confidence you feel during this period.

Then comes a test, that first time when you make a choice and it turns out to not be so wise. It may be a failed relationship that, in your new flush of excitement you rushed into, only to see it come crashing about you.

It may be a change in your career that turned out to not be as wonderful as you had thought. Confusion and frustration take over. What went wrong? You thought recovery was supposed to help you find the pot of gold at the end of the rainbow. Didn't you do it right?

One of the results of recovery and a strong self-esteem is the ability to understand and develop a sense of personal responsibility. This acceptance of our own foibles not only makes them feel less upsetting, but places an objectivity needed to find our way out of whatever mess we find ourselves in. Your friends will find it an endearing and courageous trait.

Beating yourself up is an old behavior pattern. Recognize it as such. No one is perfect. If you don't believe this, pull out the morning's newspaper and read it. You'll find so many people making so many mistakes that it will put yours in the right perspective. Pat yourself on the back for having the insight to recognize you have "done wrong" and the courage to "do right." Find humor in the situation and in no time you'll be telling your friends about the hole you stepped into and how you so adeptly stepped back out.

Old behavior patterns do not change overnight. Depending on the behavior, the addiction, and the severity of the original trauma, the average number of years to totally rid yourself of addictive type behavior is two to five. Do not be alarmed if you slip in your resolve to make only healthy choices. Now is the time to stay grounded and in touch with the inner strengths you have liberated with so much work. Take a deep breath, find some quiet time to listen to your inner voices and remember the Tenth Step—*We continued to take personal inventory and when we were wrong, promptly admitted it.*

That's what the steps are for. They are your friends, your mentors, and all you need do to find your balance is read them over one more time. Another great tool is the serenity prayer: *God grant me the serenity to accept the things I cannot change, the courage to change the things I can and the wisdom to know the difference.*

Pull out your by now worn copy of REPAIR and locate the section on help in the middle of your journey. Go back and read your Magic Mirror. It is not a good idea to dismantle it immediately; you'll need it in the months to come. If you've done the program right, you'll discover that you now have the tools to handle these little speed bumps in life. Take refresher courses now and then with a seminar on self-esteem, a new book, tape, or CD you've heard about, or just go back and listen to the old ones. When we become shaky, it's helpful to get reinforcement from the original sources that got us on the right track. You'll bounce back in no time, eventually discovering that what seemed like poor choices were in fact tests that, rather than weakening you, will strengthen you. Facing fear brings strength and lessens the fear.

Taking life one day at a time is important. All you really have is the present anyway. If you do some planning, use your head, and listen to your inner voices, taking life one day at a time will come automatically. Turning any large worries over to your Higher Power helps. Twelve Steppers talk about turning problems over and then grabbing them back. The need to control our own environment is one we keep slipping back into. All you learned may feel like a double-edged sword. Aren't we supposed to take charge of our own life? Use the serenity prayer as a guide.

Another guideline is a reality check. If what you're trying to control is your stuff, that's one thing. But if it's another person's, let it alone. Why would anyone want to take on another's opportunities for growth? In doing so, you deprive them of the joy of growing in that area, while distracting yourself from your own growth. Once you've gone through a few tests, you'll find that the challenges are not so difficult to overcome, and as time goes on you'll have fewer.

Keep in mind that you followed a certain path for many years. That path contained responses that got you in a lot of trouble. Now you've learned new and better responses, but they too will take time to develop until they become automatic. We are creatures of habit. Be patient.

In taking life one day at a time, you'll also enjoy it more. All the things you didn't notice previously—sunsets and sunrises; the smile on a child's face; new recipes in the Food Section of your paper; a friendly neighbor who offers a hand; the smell of new mown grass—will now be daily occurrences. You'll learn to savor the moments. This is the way life was meant to be. Abundance will follow your days, accompanied by a feeling of finding the calm in the center of any storm that prior to recovery seemed far beyond your reach.

Previously, you may have been so codependent that only felt comfortable in the company of others. Now that you've worked your way through REPAIR and have discovered your own wonderfulness, you'll realize the joy of solitude. When you thought you had no value, there was little interest in being alone. At times it was terrifying. Only outside distractions kept you from having to face that reality. For those of you who are single, your newfound desire to enjoy your own company will not only give you a feeling of being centered, it will decrease your anxiety for a mate. In time, you'll see that if one comes along, you'll be ready; if not, you're so busy having a great time by yourself that it won't matter. This is not to say that if finding someone to grow old with is part of your dream, you should give it up. You can still make yourself available to meet new people. But once you do, you won't feel so frantic about it, and an even greater blessing occurs; you'll pull in healthier people. John Bradshaw talks about the woman who kept getting date-raped and when asked where she went to meet men, responded, *biker bars.* You will no longer be tempted to go to a biker bar or anyplace else where you meet the wrong kind of person.

As you learn to set new boundaries, others will respect them. The ones that don't will wander off to find a more willing victim. Keep in mind that an unhealthy person cannot survive long in a healthy environment and vice versa.

Now that you've eliminated your negativity and are surrounding yourself with optimism, you'll be surprised how different your world will be. Doors will open, parking spaces vacate, solutions to problems jump in front of you, and new people will come into your life to enhance it and further your own causes. Positive energy attracts positive, and negative energy pulls in negative. Unhealthy people will no longer want to be near you. That's great. And your new-found confidence will pull in winners.

Now you can set your mind to other things. One of the most important is learning about goal setting. You have the rest of your life in front of you. What do you want to do with it—especially now that you know how to make healthy choices?

Pretend that everything you want is yours for the asking. Then make a list of all of them. Leave nothing off. Why not dream big? If you're not sure what direction you want to head in, do some research. Brainstorm your interests. Are you happy with your job? Why not? What would you like to do instead? How would you get there? Be realistic. If you're in your 60s, can't hold a tune, and always wanted to be a world famous opera singer, that may be outside your reach. But in a world filled with potential, there must be something that is not. It's never too late to go back to school. Age can only improve some occupations—writing, for example.

Explore ideas, follow threads, go to a bookstore and see what interests attract you. Do more writing, more brain-storming. Talk to friends who are accomplishing goals and ask them how they're doing it. Many motivational recordings and books are available. Remember that repetitive listening is the key.

There is not only a solution for every problem; there is an adventure for every boredom. *Auntie Mame,* in the novel of the same name by Patrick Dennis, said, "Life is a banquet and most poor suckers are starving to death." What would you like at your banquet and why are you going hungry?

Take a look at all aspects of your life. Then write down whether or not you are satisfied with them. If not, write down possible changes you could make. Use the following exercise as a guideline:

**Personal relationships:** ____Satisfied ____Not Satisfied

What I can do to change it?_____

_____

**Career Choice:** ____Satisfied ____Not Satisfied

What I can do to change it?_____

_____

**Residence:** ____Satisfied ____Not Satisfied

What I can do to change it?_____

_____

**Hobbies and Interests:** ____Satisfied ____Not Satisfied

What I can do to change them?_____

_____

**List other aspects of your life and ways to change them.**

_____

_____

_____

_____

_____

Now make the following lists:

**Things I always wished I could do but never did:**

_____

_____

_____

_____

_____

**Ways I can accomplish each one of them:**

_____

_____

_____

_____

_____

Your world is unlikely to be perfect after recovery. Life goes on and sometimes it contains heartache and challenges. There will be deaths and financial stress; you may not find the man/woman of your dreams, and so on. But in your pre-recovery days when these things happened, it felt like the end of the world. Now you know it never was. Now you're better equipped to take things in stride. Move through the challenges, keeping in mind that each time you face one head-on, you increase your strength and purpose. _An easy task becomes difficult when done with reluctance._ Don't face life with reluctance; face it with purpose and courage. Most people die without ever having lived their dreams. At the end of the time allotted to you, the only thing you'll regret is the things you didn't do that you wanted to. Make bold moves and make every one count.

This is different from reacting. This is about thinking things through, coming up with choices, and making the appropriate ones with courage. This is about making your life the way you'd like it to be. You've been in basic training and have earned the right to be all that you can be.

Let's talk about purpose, that path in life you were meant to be on. Everyone has one, but not everyone has the ability to recognize it. The fulfillment of purpose is one of life's greatest joys. Are you any clearer about your purpose? What would you like it to be? Or are you a flower child who would like to relax and enjoy? That's fine too. The important thing is to be happy and enjoy life—our God-given right at birth. You've been side-tracked from it for too long.

*** 

One of the biggest benefits in reaching the other side of the bridge is an awareness of your physical health. While living on the dark side, concern about your physical well-being may have rated low on your list of interests. Alternately, focusing solely on physical ill health can amount to talking yourself into all sorts of new health problems. Once you've faced the demons from your past and learn to avoid stepping in the same destructive holes, you're going to take a keen interest in living a long life.

This means changing life-style habits in diet, exercise, and other preventive medicine areas. Here are a few words to guide you through these.

## Diet

Invest in a class on Nutrition. It may save your life. At the very least, take a look at the books and CDs available on the subject. Subscribe to health promotion magazines and steep yourself in information on what to eat. If your health care provider has classes on diet and nutrition, take them. Like recovery, information on good nutrition is everywhere. If you follow the guidelines of the Food Pyramid for a period of only one week, you will notice a substantial difference in your emotional well being.

## Exercise

Begin a daily regime of exercise. Check out DVDs, walk thirty minutes each day, find a local gym, or start bicycling. Decide on whatever exercise you like. This will accomplish more than one purpose. You'll meet new people of similar interests, and with the addition of good nutrition the results in your emotional stability are dramatic.

## Dental Care

When is the last time you had your teeth checked? How good are you at flossing and regular brushing? Do you really want false teeth by the age of 50? Call your dentist and put yourself on a regular program of good dental hygiene.

## Preventive Medicine Regulars

Many yearly exams are available for preventing possible serious health problems. An annual check-up which includes a pap smear and mammogram for women and a prostate exam for men is essential. As you grow older, there are more extensive exams such as a colonoscopy, bone density tests, and others. Look into these. If you're diabetic, have hypertension, or high cholesterol, it may be a good time to make changes on how you deal with these. If you smoke, you may finally have the courage to quit. Smoking is sometimes a way of distracting our- selves from the pain of that inner child. Once you bring happiness to that child, she won't need a cigarette in her hand to cope. Since you're now living in a new world, make it a healthy one.

## Good Grooming

One who looks good, feels good. How long have you been telling yourself you're going to get a new hairdo or invest in a manicure? How about a facial or a regular pedicure? You don't need to spend a lot of money to be- gin taking care of the cosmetic side to your body. A simple foot massage after a bubble bath in the evening is a way of pampering yourself with good grooming. Take more care with your makeup; find more stylish and flat- tering ways to dress. If you have a few pounds that need to disappear, you're more apt to do this in the post re- covery period.

***

I hope REPAIR has proven beneficial in changing your life and I am grateful for the opportunity to help you on your journey. The things you have learned in this pro- gram are life changing tools. Avail yourself of them on a daily basis. You have finally recognized that the most important person in your world is you, a whole new you, one who is going to be a part of all the wonderful things waiting on the other side of that bridge.

| Appendix | **Resources** |  |

## The Desiderata by Max Ehrmann

"Go placidly amidst the noise and haste and remember what peace there may be in silence. As far as possible, without surrender, be on good terms with all persons. Speak your truth quietly and clearly and listen to others, even the dull and ignorant for they too have their story. Avoid loud and aggressive persons, for they are vexations to the spirit.

If you compare yourself with others you may become vain or bitter; for always there will be greater and lesser persons than yourself. Enjoy your achievements as well as your plans. Keep interested in your own career, however humble; it is a real possession in the changing fortunes of time.

Exercise caution in your business affairs; for the world is full of trickery. But let this not blind you to what virtue there is; many people strive for high ideals; and everywhere life is full of heroism. Be yourself. Especially, do not feign affection. Neither be cynical about love; for in the face of all aridity and disenchantment it is perennial as the grass.

Take kindly the counsel of the years, gracefully surrendering things of youth. Nurture strength of spirit to shield you in sudden misfortune. But do not distress yourself with imaginings. Many fears are born of fatigue and loneliness.

Beyond a wholesome discipline, be gentle with yourself. You are a child of the universe, no less than the trees and the stars; you have a right to be here. And whether or not it is clear to you, no doubt the universe is unfolding as it should.

Therefore be at peace with God, whatever you conceive Him to be, and whatever your labors and aspirations, in the noisy confusion of life keep peace with your soul.

With all its sham, drudgery and broken dreams, it is still a beautiful world. Be careful. Strive to be happy."

## The Twelve Steps

1. We admitted we were powerless over others and that our lives had become unmanageable.

2. We came to believe that a power greater than ourselves could restore us to sanity.

3. We made a decision to turn our lives over to the care of God as we understood God.

4. We made a fearless and searching moral inventory of ourselves.

5. We admitted to God, to ourselves, and to another human being the exact nature of our wrongs.

6. We were entirely ready to have God remove all these defects of character.

7. We humbly asked God to remove our shortcomings.

8. We made a list of people we had harmed and became willing to make amends to them all.

9. We made direct amends wherever possible, except when to do so would harm them or others.

10. We continued to take personal inventory and when we were wrong, promptly admitted it.

11. We sought through prayer and meditation to improve our conscious contact with God, praying only for knowledge of his will and the power to carry it out.

12. Having had a spiritual awakening as a result of these steps, we tried to carry this message to others and to practice these principles in all our affairs.

## The Serenity Prayer

God, grant me the serenity

to accept the things

I cannot change,

the courage

to change the things I can,

and the wisdom to know

the difference.

# The Optimist's Creed

I Promise:

To be so strong that nothing can disturb my peace of mind.

To talk health, happiness and prosperity to every person I meet.

To make all my friends feel there is something special in them.

To look at the sunny side of everything and make my optimism come true.

To think only of the best, to work only for the best, and expect only the best.

To be just as enthusiastic about the success of others as I am about my own.

To forget the mistakes of the past and press on to the greater achievement of the future.

To wear a cheerful countenance at all times and give every living creature I meet a smile.

To give so much time to the improvement of myself that I have no time to criticize or judge others.

To be too large for worry, too noble for anger, too strong for fear and too happy to permit the presence of trouble.

From *Your Forces and How to Use Them* by Christian D. Larson (1912).

# Support Groups

## Twelve Step Programs

For the phone number of a Twelve Step Program your area of the USA, call 1-800-555-1212, and ask for the Program of your choice below and the phone number of the nearest branch location.

- Alcoholics Anonymous
- Al-anon
- Co-Dependents Anonymous
- Overeaters Anonymous
- Narcotics Anonymous

## Suggested Websites

www.catharsisfoundation.org Catharsis Foundation is a non-profit incorporated in Calgary Alberta in 2004 for survivors of ALL forms of child abuse—internationally

www.thelamplighters.org The Lamplighters is a movement founded by Marjorie McKinnon, author of *RE-PAIR Your Life*, for survivors of incest and child sexual abuse. Emphasizes the importance of REPAIRing the damage done and recommends using the program RE-PAIR as a model for recovery.

www.angelashelton.com Angela Shelton is a public speaker, author, actress, writer and advocate for victims of child sexual abuse.

www.mskinnermusic.com Mike Skinner offers Hope, Healing & Help for Trauma, Abuse & Mental Health through music, resources and advocacy

www.familywatchdog.us A website that lists names and addresses of all known sex offenders in the US.

www.preventchildabuse.org Since 1972, *Prevent Child Abuse America* has led the way in building awareness, providing education and inspiring hope to everyone involved in the effort to prevent the abuse and neglect of our nation's children.

www.rainn.org *The Rape, Abuse & Incest National Network* is the nation's largest anti-sexual assault organization and has been ranked as one of "America's 100 Best Charities" by *Worth* magazine.

www.recoverybooks.com The recovery and self-help bookstore.

www.prevent-abuse-now.com This website, also called *Pandora's Box* offers information, offenses, prevention and protection regarding child sexual abuse.

www.acestudy.org The *Adverse Childhood Experiences Study* is an ongoing collaboration between the Centers for Disease Control and Prevention and Kaiser Permanente. It is perhaps the largest scientific research study of its kind, analyzing the relationship between multiple categories of childhood trauma (ACEs), and health and behavioral outcomes later in life.

www.stopcsa.org The goal of *Stop The Silence* is to stop child sexual abuse and related forms of violence by changing societal relationships among and between groups.

www.childmolestationprevention.org *The Child Molestation Research & Prevention Institute* is a national science-based nonprofit organization dedicated to preventing child sexual abuse through research, education, and family support.

www.darkness2light.org *Darkness to Light* is a national nonprofit organization and initiative that seeks to diminish the incidence and impact of child sexual abuse, so that more children will grow up healthy and whole

# Bibliography

## A suggested list of books (for recovery)

Adams, E. (1994). *Understanding the trauma of childhood psycho-sexual abuse.* Bedford, MA: Mills & Sanderson.

Bass, E., & Davis, L. (1994). *The courage to heal, 3rd Ed.* New York: Collins.

Bass, E. & Thornton, L. (1991) *I never told anyone: writings by women survivors of child sexual abuse.* New York: Harper.

Beattie, M. (2001). *Codependent no more: how to stop controlling others and start caring for yourself.* Hazelden Publishing & Educational Services.

Beattie, M. (1989). *Beyond codependency and getting better all the time.* New York: HarperCollins.

Bradshaw, J. (1990). *The family: a new way of creating solid self-esteem.* New York: HCI.

Bradshaw, J. (2005). Healing the Shame that Binds You: Recovery Classics Edition. New York: HCI.

Bradshaw, J. (1992). *Homecoming: reclaiming and healing your inner child.* New York: Bantam.

Dyer, W. (1994). Pulling your own strings: dynamic techniques for dealing with other people and living your life as you choose. New York: HarperTorch.

Forward, S. & Buck, C. (2002). *Toxic parents: overcoming their hurtful legacy and reclaiming your life.* New York: Bantam.

Lerner, H. (2005). *The dance of anger: a woman's guide to changing the patterns of intimate relationships.* New York: Harper.

Lerner, H. (1990). *The dance of intimacy.* New York: Harper.

Jeffers, S. (2006). *Feel the fear and do it anyway.* New York: Ballantine.

Kellogg, T. (1990), *Broken toys broken dreams: understanding and healing codependency, compulsive behaviors and family.* Brat Inc.

Leman, K., & Carlson. (1990). *Unlocking the secrets of your childhood memories.* New York: Pocket Books.

Maltz, W. (2001). *The sexual healing journey: a guide for survivors of sexual abuse, Revised Ed.).* New York: Collins.

Middleton-Moz, J. (1989). *Children of trauma: rediscovering your discarded self.* New York: HCI.

Norwood, R. (1994). *Women who love too much.* New York: Pocket Books.

Russianoff, P. (1981). *Why do i think i am nothing without a man?* New York: Bantam.

Sanford, P. (1988). *Healing victims of sexual abuse.* New York: Victory.

Smith, M. (1985). *When i say no, i feel guilty.* New York: Bantam.

## A Suggested List of Books (For Post-Recovery)

Borysenko, J. (2007), *Minding the body, mending the mind, revised ed.* New York: Da Capo Lifelong Books.

Chopra, D. (1994). *The seven spiritual laws of success: a practical guide to the fulfillment of your dreams.* New York: New World Library.

Colgrove, Bloomfield & McWilliams. (1993). *How to survive the loss of a love.* Los Angeles: Prelude Press.

Dwinell, L. & Middleton-Moz, J. (1986). *After the tears: reclaiming the personal losses of childhood.* New York: HCI.

Frankl, V. (1997). *Man's Search for Meaning, Rev. / Updated Ed.* New York: Pocket Books

Hammarskjold, D. *Markings* (2006). New York: Vintage.

Lindbergh, A. (1941). *Gift from the sea.*

Markova, D. (1991). *The art of the possible: a comprehensive approach to understanding the way people think, learn and communicate.* New York: Weiser.

McWilliams & John-Roger. (1995). *You can't afford the luxury of a negative thought.* Los Angeles: Prelude Press.

Moore, T. (1994). *Care of the soul : a guide for cultivating depth and sacredness in everyday life.* New York: Harper Perennial.

Moore, T. (1994). *Soul Mates: Honoring the mysteries of love and relationship.* New York: Harper Perennial.

Peck, S. (1988). *The road less traveled.* New York: Rider & Co.

## A Suggested List of Audiobooks (For Recovery)

Bradshaw, John, *The Family*

Bradshaw, John, *Healing The Shame That Binds You*

Beattie, Melody, *Codependent No More*

Beattie, Melody, *Beyond Codependency*

## A Suggested List of Audiobooks (for post recovery)

Bradshaw, John, *Creating Love*

Bradshaw, John, *The Next Great Stage of Growth*

Canfield, Jack, *Self-esteem and Peak Performance*

Peale, Norman Vincent, *The Power of Positive Thinking*

Peale, Norman Vincent, *Positive Imaging*

Robbins, Anthony, *Unlimited Power*

Ziglar, Zig, *Goals: Setting & Achieving Them on Schedule*

These lists are only suggestions for starting your journey and not, by any means, the only ones available. Your local bookstore and library contain a wealth of recovery books and recordings.

## About the Author

In 1988, prompted by se-
vere depression and resurf-
acing memories, Marjorie
McKinnon entered a program
for recovery from incest, a
journey that took almost five
years to complete. During
that time, she wrote about
her experience, a chronicle of
going from a place of despair
to one of joy. That book, titled *Let Me Hurt You and
Don't Cry Out* was her first
attempt to get published.

Unable to sell it, she spent the next five years developing a program on recovery from child sexual abuse.
Despite being a non-professional, it was her belief that a
program devised by someone who had walked the same
road would be a sensitive and pragmatic resource. She
titled that self-published book, *REPAIR: A Program for
Recovery from Incest & Childhood Sexual Abuse* and used
it as an accompaniment to seminars she taught in the
Los Angeles area.

In the last ten years, Marjorie has completed a fiction
trilogy that follows the life of Kathleen McGuire whose
spirit guide, Jake, provides her with wisdom and direction from another world as she gets herself in and out of
trouble. Three nonfiction works, *Mystical Experiences:
Tales of The Inner Light, Blue Skies and Green Lights:
How to Create a Perfect World Through Positive Growth in
The Six Dimensions,* a post-recovery book, and *A Com-*

*mon Sense Spiritual Path,* as well as a mystery novel, *When First We Practice to Deceive* and a fiction work titled: *Here Lies,* are all completed. *Hello, My Name is Marjorie,* close to completion, is a sprightly and often humorous email account of her courtship with Tom McKinnon, her husband, whom she met on the Internet while doing genealogy research for the McKinnon clan (her name was also McKinnon). Another novel, *After The Rain,* and a nonfiction work called, *Our Greatest Asset: The Elderly* are works in progress.

Marjorie is currently doing speaking engagements in the northern Arizona area and is the founder of *The Lamplighters,* a movement for victims of child sexual abuse that emphasizes the importance of REPAIRing the damage. Feeling that a movement of one voice would give more power to survivors, she hopes one day to have Lamplighters all over the world. Currently, there are 32 chapters in 21 states, one chapter in Tokyo, Japan, two in Ontario, Canada and one in Plymouth, England. The interest in people wanting to start chapters is daily. If you would like to find the nearest one or consider starting your own chapter, then please take a few moments to visit the Lamplighter's website: http://TheLamplighters.org.

# Index

## A

addictions, 40, 150
alcoholic, 1, 5, 7, 19, 33, 45, 49,
    90, 114
    parent, 113
anger, 23, 53
anxiety, viii, 5, 39, 153
Awareness
    properties, 103

## B

belief system, 120, 121, 146
bipolar, 43
boundaries, 33, 37
boundary setting, 96–99
boundary violation, 15, 91, 92
Bradshaw, J., 9, 48, 70, 87, 94,
    133, 153, 171, 174
Bridge of Recovery, 6, 9, 13, 21,
    70, 139
bulimia, 7, 42
bullying, 10, 19

## C

caffeine, 66, 67
childhood sexual abuse, ii, viii,
    1, 11, 13, 19, 22, 24, 26, 32,
    42, 55, 98, 103, 106, 121,
    130, 132, 137
    non-family, 50
    profile, 33
    re-enacting, 51
    staying present, 40
    warning signs, 31
children. See also wounded
    child
    of incest victim, 7
codependent, 62, 127
co-dependents
    characteristics, 110
commitment, 64–65
control, 35
cynicism, 53

## D

Dennis, P., 154
depression, viii, 21, 33, 44, 53,
    137, 175
diet, 158

## E

eating disorder, 42
Emerson, R.W., 100
emotional abuse, 61
emotional threats, 61
exercise, 158

## F

family history
    boundary violators, 115
    creating, 89–93
family systems, 107–14
feelings, 99–100, 105
flashbacks, 3, 48
foresight, 106
forgiveness, 129

## G

gratitude, 94
grooming, 159
guilt, 16

## H

healing, 26
hyper-vigilance, 31, 47
hypnotherapy, 83–84

## I

inappropriate affection, 130
incest
    defined, 15
    epidemic, 19
    father, 112
incest survivors, vii
inner child, 100–102

inner voices, 39, 57, 88, 96,
    122, 123, 135, 149, 150, 151
insomnia, 33, 35

**J**

Journalizing, 81
judgmental, 35, 145

**K**

knowledge, 104, 105

**L**

lies, 22

**M**

Magic Mirror, 6, 73–75, 80, 151
    messages, 75–79
memories, 31
Missildine, W.H., 9
molested
    boundaries, 37
    healing from, 27
    traits, 117

**N**

needy, 36
negative energy, 17, 18, 77,
    129, 153
nightmares, 4, 35

**O**

obedient partner, 109
obesity, 46
obsessive-compulsive, 35
oldest daughter, 4, 11, 113
overeating, 16, 42

**P**

partner
    ideal, 38
patriarchal family, 108–9
people-pleasing, 34
perpetrator
    letter to, 93
Process, 56
promiscuity, 1, 16, 46, 71

parent, 49
prudence, 104, 105

**R**

rape, 8, 15, 47
real love, 124
recovery, 19, 63
relationships
    unhealthy, 38
religiously regimented
    household, 111–13
REPAIR
    stages, 13
rescuing, 34

**S**

self-esteem, 16, 17, 21, 33, 36,
    37, 38, 46, 48, 72, 141
self-loathing, 17, 120
shame, 16, 24
sleep, 66
sleep problems, 31, 35
Socrates, 103
songs, 94
stubbornness, 137
subliminal messages, 119
suicide, 33, 36, 63, 71
support, 59–63

**T**

therapy
    group, 56–57
    individual, 56
tolerance, 54
toxic people, 139
trust, 95–96
Twelve Step Programs, 48, 56,
    57, 167
    honesty, 138
    working, 89

**V**

visualization, 104

**W**

wounded child, 19, 23, 38, 52,
    96, 106, 116, 137, 141

Breinigsville, PA USA
09 May 2010
237564BV00002B/10/P